What Does Christ Want?

What Does Christ Want?

ABRIDGED EDITION

Bernard Haring, C. Ss. R.

AVE MARIA PRESS
Notre Dame, Indiana 46556

NIHIL OBSTAT:
   John L. Reedy, C.S.C.
   Censor Deputatus

IMPRIMATUR:
   ✠ Most Rev. Leo A. Pursley, D.D.
   Bishop of Ft. Wayne-South Bend

Complete English translation published by
Alba House, Staten Island, N. Y. 10314

241.5

CONTENTS

Preface

The present book integrates the articles which I published during the year 1967 in *Ave Maria* magazine and *Famiglia Cristiana* magazine. The intention was to give an integrated perspective on Christian morality in a way that even those not trained in school theology should be able to profit. I kept all intelligent Christians in mind.

I want to express my gratitude to the translator, Albert Wimmer, and my sister, Sister Luvidia Haering, and Sister Jean Gabrielle and Mrs. Josephine McDonald Bryan, who helped me in the final revision of the English text.

Bernard Häring, C.Ss.R.

Introduction

In these essays on "What Does Christ Want?" I would like to take my readers to the mountain of the beatitudes and into the room of the Last Supper. There we want to look at the Lord, listen to His words, and meditate on His "Happy are you." Through the "Good News" addressed to us, we shall try to understand what the Lord expects of us here and now. He is the giver of our law; He is the way, the truth and the life.

Let us forget for a while all our daily cares so we can listen intently to the Good News and the moral message of the Lord. Soon we will realize, however, that there is room for the images of our daily life in the clear air on the mountain of the beatitudes. For the Lord takes us infinitely seriously *just as we are* as soon as we take Him seriously for His own sake. He has a message for us which sheds light on our questions about life and on our sphere of existence: "You are the light of the world" (Matt. 5:14).

The chapters in this book are intended to be a contribution toward the postconciliar renewal of our lives. This renewal requires that we totally surrender to the spirit of the Gospel, so that we may face our world with the right spirit and thus bring salvation to it; it also implies that we listen to the "signs of the times," which we can interpret only to the extent that we look and listen to Christ who makes the Good News of the heavenly kingdom known to us.

When Christianity was still the axis of our culture — and faith was still unquestioningly accepted as the norm for our thoughts and deeds—it was less harmful to summarize the bare commandments and duties of Christians in catechism and sermons and in education and in spiritual guidance, without having to point constantly to the fundamentals of faith.

Today the situation is different. We are living in a world where a variety of ideologies and philosophies of life also produce differences in moral concepts. As Christians we have to become more aware of what it means to be a Christian if we are to avoid simple assimilation of ourselves to the *Zeitgeist* (spirit of the age). We must be in a position to justify our faith and the foundation of our morality to ourselves and to our neighbors and fellow citizens. This must be complemented by honest ecumenical concern. We Christians must all be equally at home in the world of Holy Scripture—the basis for a better understanding of one another—so that, together, we may make known and witness to the world Our Lord Jesus Christ and His moral message.

The following presentation of Christian morality does not take the Ten Commandments of the law of the Old Covenant as its point of departure. The center of our Christian life is *Christ*. We must first listen to His sermon as handed down to us by the inspired authors of the New Testament. The place of the Old Testament's Sinai law—the Ten Commandments—is of secondary importance in a truly Christian approach. It will become clear to every reader that it is impossible to simply ignore the Ten Commandments; but we should not consider them only in their imperfect Old Testament form. That

8

which was present in a hidden way in the Old Testament does not become completely known until the New Covenant. The moral teaching of the New Testament is of a beauty which, in comparison to the Decalogue, could not have been envisioned prior to it.

In keeping with the tradition of Catholic moral theology we shall also speak of commandments and virtues. But the decisive angle shall be the Sermon on the Mount (Matt. 5-7) and the farewell discourses of Jesus (John 13-17). This will show us that there is more to Christian life than just commandments and virtues. But at the same time both commandments and virtues will appear all the more lovable and obligatory the more they appear in the light of the Good News.

Is the Sermon on the Mount merely a collection of pious admonitions which carry no obligation? Or does it offer us detailed solutions to concrete questions which we can apply, without too much difficulty, to our own lives? Does it give us legal directives valid for all times and places? Answers to such questions are of fundamental importance to the understanding of Christian morals.

The Beatitudes

How happy are the poor in spirit:

theirs is the kingdom of heaven.

Happy the gentle:
they shall have the earth for their heritage.

Happy those who mourn:
they shall be comforted.

Happy those who hunger and thirst for what is
right:
they shall be satisfied.

Happy the merciful:
they shall have mercy shown them.

Happy the pure in heart:
they shall see God.

Happy the peacemakers:
they shall be called sons of God.

Happy those who are persecuted in the cause of
right:
theirs is the kingdom of heaven.

I
The Commandment of Love

Seven times in the Sermon on the Mount the Lord begins with the phrase: "But I tell you." The number seven symbolizes "fullness." In this case it expresses the fullness of the authority of Jesus: He teaches the law of the New Covenant with authority. When He says "For I tell you" for the seventh time, His entire teachings are summed up fully and finally. It is the commandment of perfection, the call to imitate the love of the heavenly Father: "Love your enemies and pray for those who persecute you; in this way you will be sons of your Father in heaven, for he causes his sun to rise on bad men as well as on good, and his rain to fall on honest and dishonest men alike. For if you love those who love you, what right have you to claim any credit? Even the tax collectors do as much, do they not? And if you save your greetings for your brothers, are you doing anything exceptional? Even the pagans do as much, do they not? You must therefore be perfect just as your heavenly Father is perfect" (Matt. 5:44-48). We do not truly become children of the heavenly Father until we try to make His merciful and all-encompassing love the basis of our life.

Essentially, then, the call to holiness means nothing else but the call to compassionate, sympathetic and active love of one's neighbor in accord with the ideal and the example of God. The emphasis apparently lies on compassion. St. Luke, in his shorter wording of the Sermon on the

Mount, interprets the commandment, "Be perfect," very briefly with the words: "Be compassionate as your Father is compassionate" (Luke 6:36). The most important thing for a Christian is to believe wholeheartedly and to recognize by his life that God is love, and that He has created and redeemed us for the purpose of loving Him and, with Him and through Him, our neighbor. God reveals to us His countenance, the ways of His love; thus He reveals to us the true face of a love which represents the fullness of Christian morality.

"Show Us the Father"

Our heavenly Father reveals to us the ways of His love because He really and truly wants to make us His sons. If we know Him, our conduct will reflect our identity as His sons and daughters. Philip says to Jesus: "Lord, let us see the Father and then we shall be satisfied" (John 14:8). Jesus replies: "To have seen me is to have seen the Father. . . . You must believe me when I say that I am in the Father and the Father is in me" (John 14:9-11). The great mission of the Incarnate Word aims at making completely known His Father's love on earth. This is emphasized by the introductory verses to chapters 13-17 of the Gospel according to St. John which are the ultimate and greatest tenets of Christian morality in Holy Scripture. "He had always loved those who were his in the world, but now he was to show the full extent of his love" (John 13:1). The Father's plan of salvation is to choose us as His sons and daughters through His beloved and only-begotten Son. He loves us together with His

Son and through His Son. The Son passes on the love of the Father to us. "As the Father has loved me, so I have loved you" (John 15:9). In His infinite love for us, Christ is the visible image of the invisible God (cf. Col. 1:15; II Cor. 4:4). Through Him we truly come to a knowledge of God's love for us.

Because Jesus has revealed the love of the heavenly Father unto His death on the cross, He can also restate the commandment of the Sermon on the Mount in the new law of His farewell, "Be perfect as your heavenly Father," without any change in meaning: "This is my commandment: love one another as I have loved you" (John 15:12). The imitation of Christ entails the imitation of the heavenly Father in His compassionate love.

The love of Jesus for us is the love of the Redeemer, that is, a compassionate love that brings salvation. "A man can have no greater love than to lay down his life for his friends" (John 15:13). However, we are not the friends of Jesus by nature. Because of sin we were rather considered the enemies of God. Thus the love of Jesus until His death on the cross is love for His enemies: not only those who were instrumental in His crucifixion, but also those for whose sake He died on the cross. We can be His friends only because through infinite compassion He has chosen us as His friends. "You did not choose me, no, I chose you" (John 15:16). Ultimately the love of the Redeemer reshapes us in such a way that we truly become sons of God before all men. It becomes evident that the fruit of redemption and the true result of Christian morals are that we make the heavenly Father and Christ known to all men through our love. "In the same way, your light must shine in the sight of men, so that, seeing your good works, they may give the praise to your Father in heaven" (Matt. 5:16). Good works encompass everything that originates from a loving heart and makes known the true face of love.

In this context we understand the veneration of the saints. We look up in gratitude to the true disciples of Christ who make the imitation of Christ, and consequently the imitation of the heavenly Father, believable and concrete in ever-new historical relationships. The calling of all men to holiness implies, above all, the command to make the love of God intelligible to one another, helping one another to visualize it. Gratitude for our neighbor's love for us and our own daily striving to become for him a reflection of God's kindness, sharpen our vision of the love of the invisible God who wants to become visible in Christ and in all our brothers. "We ourselves saw and we testify that the Father sent his Son as saviour of the world. . . . We ourselves have known and put our faith in God's love toward ourselves. God is love and anyone who lives in love lives in God, and God lives in him" (I John 4:14-16). Because Jesus revealed to the world the love of the Father and because He chose us for His disciples and friends, we can say: "Even in this world we have become as He is" (I John 4:17). We are privileged to spread the news of God's love, thus experiencing our greatest hope in faith. Any conscious lack of brotherly love, however, obscures the image of God to our neighbor and diminishes our hope. "For how can he who does not love his brother whom he sees, love God, whom he does not see?" (I John 4:20).

This exchange of God's love is the core of spirituality in marriage. "A man . . . is the image of God and reflects God's glory" (I Cor. 11:7). However, this is only insofar as he fulfills his mission: "Husbands should love their wives just as Christ loved the Church and sacrificed himself for her" (Eph. 5:25). A husband who loves his wife in accord with the love of Christ so enriches her life that she is able to return this love. At the same time, she envisions more fully the love of Christ and that of the heavenly Father. The love given is returned as a stream of God's love and draws both the lover and the beloved closer to the love of God. "For a man to love his wife is for him to love himself" (Eph. 5:28).

With his teachings about marriage St. Paul wants to help the wife realize Christian love within the system of the patriarchal family and thus experience in humility and inner peace the great secret of love. Nevertheless, by pointing to the revelation of the love of the heavenly Father, he also provides the husband with motivation and directives which in the course of time must reshape the patriarchal system from within. A relationship between equal partners is manifest in the decisive aspect of marriage: the mutual love of wife and husband. They are called upon to attest to each other the love of God and to make it into an increasingly more meaningful experience.

This is also the core of any other calling. It is the most noble mission of a priest to announce the love of God not only in words but also through his love as brother among brothers, as the image of the heavenly Father. In gratitude he will accept the love of the faithful entrusted to him and he will return it as a servant, not as a master. Thus the priests are fathers and teachers insofar as "together with all the faithful in Christ they are disciples of the Lord" (*Decree on the Ministry and Life of Priests*, Art. 9). The celibacy of priests and members of religious orders should not mean coldness and isolation. It signifies the cordial openness of unselfish love. Both priests and religious are called upon to represent to one another in their own way what married people can be to each other: witnesses of the gracious love of God. Through their unfeigned and gentle love, they aid one another in the task of manifesting to all the faithful the calling to sainthood.

The True Face of Love

An extreme situation ethics (J. Fletcher, *Situation Ethics*) tries to justify everything—even adultery and false oaths, abortion and atom bombs on open towns—with the one principle of love. Thus "unprincipled" love appears as a sphinx, a principle without a definitive content. Should we therefore no longer speak on love or, at least, refrain from emphasizing the all-embracing character of love? By no means. Even in Jesus' time much was called love that was not truly love. However, the Lord teaches His whole doctrine in terms of love, showing us through His personality, in His example and through all His words—particularly through the Passion, death and Resurrection—the true nature of redeeming and redeemed love. The Sermon on the Mount must also be read in this perspective: It furnishes us, above all, with the criteria needed to make our judgments, to distinguish true love from its counterfeits.

The final and the sharpest test of redeemed love is love of one's enemies, the strength and firmness of love precisely at the point where we meet resistance, misunderstanding, rejection and contempt. The heathen, the tax collectors and the public sinners number among those who are usually friendly to their benefactors, friends and flatterers. The man who wants a justified claim to the honorable title of son or daughter of God has to prove his worth before his enemies and those persecuting him (Matt. 5:44-48). The love of one's neighbor not only prohibits murder but also anger and any scornful, unloving word (Matt. 5:22). He who wants to please the Father with an offering must take great pains to remove any misunderstanding and do everything possible to be reconciled with his brother when his brother has something against him (Matt. 5:23-24). Genuine and respectful love not only rules out adultery, it also guards against any adulterous desire (Matt. 5:27-28). Redeemed love shows neither weakness against oneself nor against one's neighbor; moreover, it is absolutely determined to remove everything blocking love. Redeemed love proves its worth in marital fidelity, and that implies more than avoidance of divorce. The readiness to be reconciled and to keep open every road to reconciliation even bars divorcées from remarrying (cf. Matt. 5:31-33; Matt. 19:9; Mark 10:11-12; Luke 16:18; I Cor. 7:10). True love creates a climate of mutual confidence in a spirit of absolute sincerity and truthfulness (Matt. 5:

33-37). Truly great love also reveals itself in non-violence and gentleness: in the gentle force of love.

Love is even willing to forego duly acquired rights whenever there is a possibility to win over or to convince another human being through obliging love (Matt. 5:38-42). Thus it is indeed necessary to keep together all the forces of love. As a housewife in the past watched over the fire and gathered all the red-hot coals, Christian gentleness takes every opportunity to increase and to manifest love so that with patience and gentleness, it may also win those who still resist love or find it difficult to love us. This is the meaning of the admonition, to "heap red-hot coals on his head" (Rom. 12:20). Love is consequently never satisfied with mere defense and self-defense. It is always active, always intent to help the other human person on the road to love. "Do not let evil conquer you, but defeat evil by doing good" (Rom. 12:21).

The tests of genuine love, or the instructions concerning the discernment of the spirits, are the core of the moral teachings of the New Testament. Thus the Sermon on the Mount finds its counterpart in the song of songs of love: "Love is always patient and kind; it is never jealous; love is never boastful or conceited; it is never rude or selfish; it does not take offense, and is not resentful. Love takes no pleasure in other people's sins but delights in the truth; it is always ready to excuse, to trust, to hope, and to endure whatever comes" (I Cor. 13:4-7). Together with St. Augustine one can say: "Be mindful of love and do as you please" (Commentary to the First Letter of John, tract 7 no. 8 in PL 35, 2033)—but then one must point out the true face of love. True love carries with it the entire chorus of virtues. The Apostle of the Gentiles emphasizes to the Judaists who are getting lost in the maze of their legalism: "The whole of the law is summarized in a single command: 'Love your neighbor as yourself'" (Gal. 5:14-15). But, at the same time, he is very much concerned about making it clear to everybody that true love drives out selfishness and all its poisoned doings—all mere caricatures of love. "What the Spirit brings forth is very different: love, joy, peace, patience, kindness, goodness, trustfulness, gentleness and self-control. There is no law against things like that, of course" (Gal. 5:19-23).

However, in this effort, it is crucial to recognize the true meaning of love so that we will not only possess wonderful descriptions in words, human images and ideals. We must understand that it ultimately reveals itself in the face of Christ. This is already the key to the Sermon on the Mount. It is made even clearer to us through the great synthesis which John gives in the last discourse of Jesus, who Himself teaches the true meaning of love through His personality and His example. The human words of the Incarnate Word form a wonderful unity with His incarnate countenance. Jesus teaches through the washing of feet that love is humble; in His conversation with His somewhat dense disciples He reveals the friendly love that is always patient and kind. Finally, He points to the great secret of His death: "A man can have no greater love than to lay down his life for his friends" (John 15:13).

Love Is More Than a Commandment

Love cannot actually be commanded as one orders any other outward service. The fact, however, that God actually commands love cannot be doubted when one reads the Sermon on the Mount or the farewell of Jesus. However, we shall never realize the full dynamism and force of the commandment unless we are fully aware of the mode in which God commands: that we are concerned here with something infinitely greater than a bare commandment.

Love approaches us in the form of God's self-revelation. It shines on the countenance of Christ. It spreads to us in His joyous proclamation of the Good News of love. It invades our spirit and our heart in the beatitudes as a blessed power and force emanating from God. God's love, as it illuminates and embraces the world through Christ, makes us also the light of the world. Faith is the joyous and grateful acceptance of the message of this love and it is the trusting surrender of ourselves to love as it approaches us in the Incarnate Son of God. Love is the great mystery of our faith. That is why in faith love also becomes the great commandment.

The Gospel according to St. John lays special stress on the depth and height of this mystery in which the commandment is rooted. It was not we who loved first; God loved us first. He does not only reveal His love to us externally. He imparts it to us as the new life. "I am the vine, you are the branches. He who abides in me, and I in him, he bears much fruit" (John 15:5). Love is an entirely personal call that becomes full reality only for the free man. But it is, above all, an offer. The decisive factor is the most intimate union possible with Christ, the "remaining in Him." The more we receive and embrace Him in faith and the more we surrender ourselves to Him, the more we trust in His grace and the more we look up to Him, all the more natural and joyful will the commandment be to us. The image of bearing fruit is central to the Bible. It shows the unity of faith and morals, of spirituality and morality.

The Council clearly emphasizes this point of view as decisive for the scientific presentation of Christian morals and, consequently, also for the proclamation of morals. Christian moral teaching must above all present "the loftiness of the calling of the faithful in Christ." Being and remaining in Christ is, therefore, the key to understanding the calling. It means, furthermore, that the very gifts of God urge us "to bear fruit in charity for the life of the world" (*Decree on Priestly Formation*, Art. 16).

A practical result of this basic relationship between the mystery and the commandment of love will be an emphasis on humble prayer for light, strength, joy and docility to the operations of the Holy Spirit. The Lord reminds us of this truth in the farewell discourse, when His proclamation of the law of love is followed by the promise of the Holy Spirit's assistance (John 16:5-15). He it is who helps us to know and to love Christ more and more, and thus to joyously embrace the commandment of love. The less we look on it as a bare commandment, the more we will feel urged to fulfill it with all the strength God grants us. And since we become increasingly aware of love's higher demands and of our own shortcomings the more we grow in love, we will also pray more and more, putting our trust in God's gracious help.

Questions for Further Discussion

1. How would you restate in contemporary terms the commandment to "Be perfect"? Why does the author say that the emphasis in this commandment lies on compassion?

2. How is Jesus the prime exemplar of the love of God the Father for us?

3. Explain how love is the core of any calling. What is the sharpest test of redeemed love?

4. Do we usually think of morality in terms of love? How is the whole law of God summed up in the single command to love?

5. Why does the author say that love "approaches us in the form of God's self-revelation"? Does God continue to reveal Himself in our time?

6. What helps us to look on the commandment of love as something more than a simple command? When do we begin to feel urged to love through sheer love and the strength God gives us to love?

II
Sacraments and the Formation of Life

Religions of all times and civilizations, including the present, have tended to separate worship from the realities of life. This, on the one hand, often led to empty ritualism with neither relation to life nor strength to transform morals and morality. Thus, scrupulous observance of ritual obligations may be found side by side with either a fixed set of morals accompanied by an irreligious narrow-mindedness that leaves no room for genuine affection; or, at the other extreme, an unbridled formlessness and corruption of morals. Barriers, often nearly insurmountable, are erected between the "sacred"—the "religious" values embodied in the ceremonials, or at least slavishly connected with the ceremonial—and the "profane," which constitutes the entire stream of life.

On the other hand, we frequently find a false encounter between religion and morality, in which religion simply sanctions the given morals—dubious and imperfect though they be—without really inspiring and transforming them in the spirit of worship of God.

Christ put an end to both the separation and the false encounter of religion and morality. This does not mean that Christianity would not face the same temptations again at a later time. But Christ teaches us, through example and word, that worship, genuine love for God (religion), is to bear fruit in active brotherly love.

Because religion and priesthood are so closely related, Christ's priesthood is also the pattern for the reciprocal relationship between religion and morals, between "sacrament" and the formation of life. Christ, the eternal high priest, is not of the priestly family of Aaron, not of the tribe of Levi; He is not a priestly official. His priesthood is entirely a "worship in spirit and in truth" (John 4:24), and He attends to His priestly calling at the tree of the cross, in His dedication to His brothers, in the manifestation of His love and in the proclamation of the Good News. Worship, the loving acceptance of the will of the heavenly Father, and the all-embracing love for man are perfectly united in His life and death. We may say that Christ predicted that the "priesthood" of officials and ritualists would be judged most severely. Although He appointed priests, it was chiefly for the purpose of witnesses to faith and love and to serve the brothers by the joyous news. He does not want officials, but rather apostles who spread the Good News by word and deed and who, through their humble service, urge the "priestly people of God" to glorify Him in solidarity and through brotherly love.

Noted biblical scholars, such as J. Jeremias, believe that Jesus' moral message as summarized in the Sermon on the Mount was "rooted in life" as an instruction following Baptism, an instruction in which the infant Church emphasized the greatness of grace and man's calling to the Church as well as the expected fruits of conversion. Already in Christ's farewell address (Gospel of St. John) we find that during the Last Supper He combined moral exhortations with the institution of the Eucharist. There, mindful of His death and Resurrection, He made known the great commandment: "Love one another as I have loved you"; at the same time He promised the descent of the Holy Spirit who would give His disciples full light and strength.

The sacraments proclaim the Good News and imply the reciprocity of gifts. At every celebration of the Holy Eucharist, we proclaim the death of the Lord as the salvific event in an ever-renewed gift and challenge. The message of Our Lord's coming to us through faith: "I have died for you; I live for you and in you" likewise includes the command, "Love one another as I have loved you."

The Mass is "valid" even when the priest purposely turns his back to his brothers and mutters unintelligible words, while those present around the altar pursue their own private devotion. In such a Mass, hardly worthy of being called a celebration of the Eucharist, the proclamation of the Sermon on the Mount and the farewell speeches of Our Lord are expressed very imperfectly, if at all; indeed, such a Mass obscures the Good News for many people.

The Mass is "valid" even if both celebrant and community seek only the comfort of their own devotion, even if they do not open themselves to the command, "Love one another as I have loved you." However, what is the use of such a "validity," after all, when it is not what Christ meant it to be? The celebration of the Eucharist is meant to be a gift appealing to both the mind and the heart, a gift of the Redeemer's love calling for reciprocity of love, goodness, compassion and unity. The grace of the sacrament becomes an actual event of salvation only if the Good News and grace received prompt us to genuine love of neighbor.

The sacraments are visible, meaningful signs of the gift and the implications of the Christian calling. Both priests and laity should cooperate so that all realize the full fruits of the sacraments.

A father whose eighth child had just been born came to see the old parish priest who had baptized all his other children. This time, however, he was not satisfied with merely making an appointment for the baptismal ceremony.

"Father," he said, "several times you have preached so beautifully about the infinite value of each child and about the gift of faith that both family and community mediate to the children. Couldn't all that be emphasized a little more during the baptismal ceremony? This time my whole family, including the mother of the child, will be present at the Baptism. After all, Baptism is such a great event in our and the child's life. Many friends and relatives are invited. How about inviting the whole parish? Couldn't the baptismal ceremony occasionally take the place of the well-attended evening devotion on Sunday? Does it not imply honor, joy and responsibility for the entire Church when God entrusts to her a child reborn in Baptism? After all, the teaching about the marvelous things promised to the child during Baptism does not concern only the immediate family. Would it not be a good idea, then, for all the faithful to take an active part in the baptismal ceremony at least a few times a year, in order to renew their own baptismal vows and thereby guarantee the newly born child of God an atmosphere of faith, hope and love in the Christian community?"

With eyes filled with tears the parish priest said, "Amen! That's the way we are going to do it. All the bells shall call to the Baptism. Likewise, our joy shall find expression in communal singing."

At the Last Supper, when Christ instituted the Holy Eucharist, He gave to His disciples the new commandment of charity. They were all gathered close around Him and had truly become one family through His love. The Lord taught His disciples through the visible proof of His humble love. Christ's humble love and service are repeated, although in various forms, during the celebration of the sacraments. "Liturgical services are not private functions, but are celebrations of the Church, which is the 'sacrament of unity' " (*Constitution on the Sacred Liturgy*, Art. 26).

Baptism and Confirmation establish the Mystical Body of Christ. In their special grace and symbolic character, they are a call to the baptized and confirmed to use all his natural abilities and supernatural gifts of grace bestowed on him in the service of love. The Eucharist is the "bond of charity" (Art. 47). To open oneself up to the grace of the Eucharist implies an essentially renewed and grateful acceptance of the community and particularly the commandment of love.

In the sacrament of Penance, God's benign compassion conveys to us the most urgent command to love one another truly in forbearing and compassionate charity. In the sacrament of Matrimony, Christ meets the Christian spouses to embrace them in His bond of love and faithfulness. "He abides with them thereafter so that, just as He loved the Church and handed Himself over on her behalf, the spouses may love each other with perpetual fidelity through mutual self-bestowal. Authentic married love is caught up into divine love" (*Constitution on the Church in the Modern World,* Art. 48).

From Holy Scripture, tradition and the liturgical forms, it becomes evident that the sacraments are, at the same time, worship of God and an expression of and a call to brotherly love. In the sacraments, God glorifies Himself through His love for man; He invites and urges us to glorify Him through our joint assent. We glorify the death of Christ when, with the help of God's grace, we are determined to remove everything from our aspirations and our life which could bar or falsify love.

The sacraments teach us a real lesson on man's powerlessness to love his neighbor in a redeeming way without God's gracious help. Yet, at the same time, they also tell us that there is no salvation unless we bear fruit in love for the benefit of our fellowmen and to the praise of God. A mere Sunday Christian who barely meets the minimal demands of the law would be stirred from his complacency by a clear understanding of the true worship of God. In like manner, the activist, too busy to listen to the Word of God, should be awakened and recognize that his life is fruitless unless Christ shines upon him.

Signs of Faith and Hope

The sacraments are signs of faith. They are expressions of God's fidelity and truthfulness, as well as the Church's faith in response to God's invitation and call. In the liturgy we gratefully receive the Word of God and joyfully surrender ourselves to Him.

The deeper the roots of faith, the more joyfully the Christian will celebrate the sacraments of faith. He who remains indifferent to the celebration of the liturgy deprives himself of the strength emanating from the community of believers. The more the individual Christian, through his joyous participation, contributes to the worthy celebration of the sacraments, the greater will be the strength derived from them.

In the sacraments Christ gives His Church the assurance of His fidelity. The response of the Christian is that of hope and confidence, which proves itself genuine only to the extent of man's serious effort to reciprocate God's fidelity.

As symbols of unity, the sacraments give us the message of a hope which leads to salvation in the blessed communion of love through perfect solidarity. "Do all you can to preserve the unity of the Spirit by the peace that binds you together. There is *one Body, one Spirit,* just as you were all called into *one* and the same hope when you were called" (Eph. 4:2-4).

The sacraments, when rightly understood and celebrated, help us to break the fetters of our self-centeredness, leading us toward a genuine, selfless concern for our neighbor's salvation.

Karl Marx believed that religion would necessarily alienate man from his earthly task. Not

29

only would the pious man lose precious hours with useless religious activities, but worse yet, he would also lose his sincere interest in the social order. Yet, in reality, true piety is a powerful motive for one to capitalize on the present opportunities in the shaping of a Christian social order. It is the hope and expectation of the "new heaven and the new earth," which during the celebration of the Sacred Liturgy challenges us to a greater vigilance for the *kairos*, the opportunities of the present moment. Christian hope not only delivers us from the wrong attachments to transitory things, but likewise teaches us the value of created things as gifts from God entrusted to man for true and concrete expressions of brotherly love.

All the sacraments transmit the message of God's compassionate love as the foundation of man's hope. In Baptism we are liberated from sin. God's long-suffering patience is glorified in the sacrament of Penance. The all-holy God, in His compassionate forgiveness of our sins, expects a similar attitude in our hearts. How can we pray with confidence: "Forgive us our trespasses," if we make no efforts to be compassionate ourselves as the Father in Heaven: "as we forgive those who trespass against us" (Luke 6:36; Matt. 6: 12)? "Yes, if you forgive others their failings, your heavenly father will forgive you yours; but if you do not forgive others, your father will not forgive your failings either" (Matt. 6:14).

If the Good News of God's compassionate love as revealed through Jesus Christ does not totally change our lives, then our hopes will be in vain. The Sermon on the Mount is very specific on this point and completely in line with the preaching of the Prophets who, in dealing with the ritualists, again and again emphasized compassion as the only sacrifice pleasing to God. "Do not judge, and you will not be judged; because the judgments you give are the judgments you will get, and the amount you measure out is the amount you will be given. Why do you observe the splinter in your brother's eye and never notice the plank in your own?" (Matt. 7:1-3). Our brothers' worst offenses are no more than splinters in comparison with our offenses against the merciful and all-holy God. How could hardhearted man, unwilling to release his brother from the debt of a few pennies, hope for compassion from the heavenly Father? It was God who first revealed His grace to us. In turn, His merciful kindness becomes for us the law of holiness so that we, too, may show mercy and compassionate love.

Each sign of divine compassion strengthens our hope for eternal life, but only to the degree that we are willing to learn from it. Veneration of Mary as the mother of mercy redounds to the greater glory and praise of God if her example impels us to compassion for our brother who is in need. Hardheartedness to our brothers indicates that our veneration of Mary is mere sentimentalism.

Christianity as a whole is a witness to God's grace. Accepted by God's merciful love, each Christian receives the urgent mission of witnessing to God's goodness and compassionate love—not so much by marches and public demonstrations of faith but rather by an all-embracing, nondiscriminating charity for the needy. Such a hymn as "Praise to the Lord for His Compassion Lasts Forever" has meaning only if it sharpens our ear for God's word: "I have given you an example so that you may copy what I have done to you. . . . Now that you know this, happiness will be yours if you behave accordingly" (John 13:15-17).

Worship of God in Spirit and in Truth

Jews and Samaritans were quarreling regarding the place of proper worship of God. Jesus' answer is: "But the hour will come—in fact it is here already—when true worshipers will honor the Father in spirit and in truth: that is the kind of worshiper the Father wants. God is spirit, and those who worship must worship in spirit and in truth" (John 4:23-24). Jesus Himself is so anointed with the fullness of the Spirit that He sacrifices Himself for his brethren in order to give praise to the infinite love of God. Jesus not only proclaims through words and signs that God is love; He worships the heavenly Father "in truth" by loving His friends in this world to the very last.

Liturgical, private and communal prayers are all intended to lead us to that kind of worship in which we address God "in spirit and in truth." Even if we say the "Our Father" in the privacy of our room, we are still united in the common bond of God's fatherhood. The Holy Eucharist, as well as the other sacraments, brings this same message home to us. Together with Christ, who "did not think of Himself" (Rom. 15:3), we are united before God as one family.

The love and example of Our Lord and Redeemer by which He glorified the heavenly Father invite us through Scripture, liturgy and the Word of God "to be tolerant with each other, following the example of Christ Jesus, so that united in mind and voice (we) may give glory to the God and Father of our Lord Jesus Christ" (Rom. 15:5-6).

These sentiments of unity should be expressed in the manner in which we celebrate the sacraments so that our whole life may be shaped by it and become a witness. "Through him, let us offer God an unending sacrifice of praise, a verbal sacrifice that is offered every time we acknowledge his name. Keep doing good works and sharing your resources, for these are sacrifices that please God" (Heb. 13:15-16).

Active, loving concern for the temporal wellbeing and the eternal salvation of our fellowmen is the most fitting expression of true worship of God.

Questions for Further Discussion

1. Discuss some examples of both the separation of religion and morality and the false encounter of religion and morality. Are these prevalent in the Church and the world today?

2. How did Christ counteract the temptation to divorce religious practice from everyday life? What is the difference between "witnesses" and "officials"?

3. How are the sacraments at the same time both a worship and an "expression of and call to brotherly love"?

4. Discuss Karl Marx's famed belief that religion would necessarily alienate man from his task on earth. Would that religion be true religion?

5. Is Christianity today a sign of God's grace? If it isn't all that it could be, what's the explanation?

III
Love of Neighbor and Its Expression

The greatest concern for a Christian is "to remain in the love of Jesus" just as Jesus Christ remained in the love of the Father (John 15:10). Jesus reveals to the world the full extent of His Father's love and of His own love for the Father through His mission to embrace all men in His redemptive love. Thus it is that the love of God also teaches Christ's disciples the other great commandment: "Love one another as I have loved you" (John 15:12). Adherence to this one commandment designates the discipleship of those remaining in Jesus and, with Him, in the heavenly Father. "His commandments are these: that we believe in the name of his Son Jesus Christ and that we love one another as he told us to" (1 John 3:23).

In this chapter we will see how love of neighbor is manifested in the beatitudes, in the works of mercy, in the virtues, and finally, in the commandments of the second table of the Decalogue.

Sentiment and Act

"Congratulations to those whose hearts are pure" (Matt. 5:8). If man in his innermost being is pure, if his intentions are truly aimed at his fellowman, then the love of neighbor will bring happiness to both the lover and the beloved, and this love will be blessedly transformed into an ever better understanding of the love of

God. Love is the dedication to the "you" in a spirit of respect and reverence, distance and closeness. The true sentiment of love accepts the other human being as a person, discovering the image of God even behind a mutilated face. Love seeks community, but a community of individuals who act each according to his own conscience and reasoning, a community without exploitation and equalitarian pressures. Love is benevolence but not of the condescending kind; love wants the best for the other human being because it believes in the great potentialities of the other man. Love is pregnant with hope for the fellowman because it is aware of the all-embracing love of God. If one honestly wishes the best for his fellowman, then one will also want to serve him whenever he stands in need and whenever God affords us the opportunity to succor him.

Humility is the surest path to love. "Happy are the poor in spirit" (Matt. 5:3). Whoever appears poor before God, receiving everything from His hand gratefully and humbly, will also be receptive to the love of his neighbor. And this is one of the most precious characteristics of Christian love. He who is only impressed with how much good he does, has done, or should do to others, elevates himself and in so doing, he looks down on the other man. Only he who accepts the love of others in a spirit of simplicity will succeed in giving love without humiliating others.

Love delights in truth (I Cor. 13:6) and mourns together with those in sorrow. "How blest are those who mourn; they shall find consolation" (Matt. 5:4). He who, with the help of God's grace, weeps with the sorrowful in undivided solidarity also succeeds in mourning his own sins, his offenses against God, in a redemptive way. On the contrary, he who cannot be moved by the physical, psychological and spiritual needs of his fellowman will only continue his conversation with the serpent, even in his contrition before God, entangled as he is with his egocentricity. Genuine compassion first finds expression in helpful words and ways. Already in his earthly life such a man will harvest plentiful blessings; he will comfort others and not turn himself inward to his own petty ego.

"How blest are those of a gentle spirit; they shall have the earth for their possession" (Matt. 5:5). Gentleness is the smoldering energy of love. The angry and impatient human being wastes away the energy of his being in a fruitless manner. To be sure, love can also get angry for the very reason that it takes the other human being seriously and because it wants to remove everything that could be a deterrent to the welfare and salvation of others, the community, or their rightly understood interests. Anger from true love is entirely different from the anger of the selfish and proud man. True anger is contained; it enlists the energy of love against evil in such a way that the other human being feels assured and understood in his own fight against evil. "Love is always patient and kind . . . it does not take offence, and is not resentful" (I Cor. 13: 4-5). The disciple of Christ knows that it is not right for him to pass final judgment over his neighbor. Precisely because in obedience to the Sermon on the Mount (Matt. 7:1) he never acts like the judge of his brother, he likewise detects the need that cries out for help, even when this cry for help sounds like an accusation or an unkind word.

This attitude of gentleness, patience and kindness not only applies to the relationship between persons but also to groups and communities. Thus, for instance, the renewal of the Church today will be a function of the concentrated and controlled love and energy on the part of the advocates of renewal. Faced with a group of boisterous representatives of an intransigent apathy who proclaim that a hundred years will not suffice to correct the mistakes of Pope John and the Second Vatican Council, it is our duty to remain firm in our hearts, determined to look ahead together with the Lord of history instead of looking for Him in the grave. Contamination by surging ill feelings can be avoided only by mustering all of one's energies of love and understanding to counteract them. "Resist evil and conquer it with good" (Rom. 12:21).

"Congratulations to the peacemakers; they shall be called sons of God" (Matt. 5:9). Love does not approve of foul peace. It does not concede that white is black and black is white. Just as Christ evoked the contradiction of the world, especially of the hardhearted lawyers, so also the true disciples of Christ have to fight the traditionalists and the impatient innovators at all times. But neither have they sided with the stubborn traditionalists against the revolutionaries, nor have they fought the cause of the revolutionaries against the traditionalists. Even though the total life with Christ gives rise to defamation, scorn and persecution, the peaceableness of the disciples of Christ who are faced with defamation is a sign of the Messianic peace and the effective invitation to a change of mind. The last cry of the martyr St. Stephen, "Lord, do not hold this sin against them" (Acts 7:60) was apt to convince those Jewish-Christians, who were skeptical about his progressive thinking and even somewhat hostile, that it was here that the love of Christ was victorious. This love clearly exposed the hardheartedness of the stoners. It also left a sting in the heart of the persecutor Saul, a sting that was due to overcome him.

"Congratulations to those who show mercy; mercy shall be shown to them" (Matt. 5:7). He who truly believes in the miracle of redemption will take every opportunity to praise God for His mercy. Yet, the best praise is doing unto our brother as He, the Father of all mercy through His beloved Son, has done unto us. Unfeigned, unlimited forgiveness and a compassion ready to act and sympathize with those who suffer become demands of the new justice for the redeemed, for God has justified us from pure mercy since we were, indeed, sinners. Grateful love for God liberates us from the petty, bitter concerns about our own justification and lets us hunger and thirst for that justice which God has revealed through us. This grateful love makes us also mindful of the dignity and rights of our fellowman.

The Acts of Mercy

As redeemed men, we cannot ignore the question of salvation for those to whom Christ, the only Redeemer, has not yet been announced and witnessed to credibly. The question becomes frightening when one remembers what the Council said with respect to the phenomenon of unbelief in our modern world: "Taken as a whole, atheism is not a spontaneous development, but stems from a variety of causes, including a critical reaction against religious beliefs, and in some places against the Christian religion in particular. Hence believers can have more than a little to do with the birth of atheism. To the extent that they neglect their own training in the faith, or teach erroneous doctrines, or are deficient in their religious, moral or social life, they must be said to conceal rather than reveal the authentic face of God and religion" (*Pastoral Constitution on the Church in the Modern World*, Art. 19). A thorough examination of conscience is, therefore, an absolute necessity for the charity of those redeemed in Christ. Every individual Christian, everyone, must humbly figure out how he can reveal the love of God to everybody and thus point the way to the true Faith.

Christ is the original sacrament in which the Father has perfectly revealed His love. The Church, the community of the true disciples of Christ, continues this mission by making the faith knowable through love. Therefore, in a deeper sense, we can say that those who show mercy to their suffering fellowmen and, above all, to their enemies, together with Christ become a sacramental sign which, by virtue of the power of the Holy Spirit, brings salvation to the world. Likewise, we can say that the poor, the despised, the embittered whose misery is crying out to us for help become either a sign of salvation or a cause of our downfall. Just as the thoughts of men, when confronted by Christ, bear witness to their fall or resurrection, so too, the physical and psychological sufferings of our neighbor become signs of salvation which must enter man's considerations in this life; through these signs man's eternal salvation is decided.

In this sense, then, the description of the Last Judgment (Matt. 25) hints at the answer to our question concerning how they can be saved who do not yet know Christ. Wherever genuine love approaches them, it is a gracious gift of God arousing in them the blessed possibility of gratitude and mercy toward others. By doing good according to their possibilities and under the operations of the Holy Spirit, they find Christ without realizing it. If, however, all of us who know Christ through faith did good in accordance with the fullness of the grace of God, then we would hardly encounter the phenomenon of the "anonymous Christians" who, indeed, draw nearer to Christ through their innermost sentiments without actually knowing Him. The fact that there are men outside the Church who surpass us in their merciful love is a powerful call to do penance. Only if we hearken humbly can we fulfill our mission to attest credibly to men that we believe in Christ in whom the Father has revealed the fullness of His love.

The Christian and the Meaning of Virtue

To the stoic who forever wants to sneak into our hearts in the guise of a Christian, virtue means above all self-preservation and self-perfection, if not self-aggrandizement. Other persons are referred to only insofar as they have something to do with the exaltation and promotion of one's ego. Subsequently, the stoic arrives at the following ethical principle: not to succumb to passions any more than is good for self-preservation. Among the passions, the stoic lists love and compassion.

A Christian patterns his concept of virtue after the example of Christ, the Good Samaritan: He sees his brother who is in need of help, he is moved by compassion, he dresses his wounds, lifts him onto his mount and pays off his hospital expenses. He does not calculate the extent to which his own virtue has been enriched. Virtue arrives on the back of deeds performed with the "you" in mind. The mystery of Easter proclaims this at all times: He who loses himself gains everything, and finds his true self; he who seeks himself in a selfish way—even though he might be performing good deeds—loses and corrupts his true self.

Christian virtue lies in that ability for a love which comes through the love of God: it is the ability to really look to our fellowman, to be grateful to him, to listen to his call, to walk up to him and honor him by doing him good. Christian virtue opens our eyes to God and our neighbor. This is precisely what is meant by conversion: to desert our egocentricity and to turn to the better opportunities for individuality in the service of our neighbor, self-preservation through self-denial, peace of mind through the passionate dedication to the kingdom of the all-uniting love of God.

Christian virtue manifests itself in the *search*

for truth: It wants to know God and fellowman better and better, and with this increasing knowledge of God and fellowman, to know oneself better in order to love ever more truthfully. Love is truthful; for, without the genuineness and truthfulness of the word, the bridge between the "you" and the "I" has no chance of holding up and it becomes undependable.

Love cannot simply be equated with *justice*; for love is above all a harmony of hearts, the personal relationship between "I," "you" and "we." Justice has reference to objective things and rights; it is meant to regulate the parity of give-and-take, the external order of the community and its structures. Zeal for these orders, for laws and rights is, however, genuine virtue only insofar as persons and community respond to the call to love and help one another become more and more capable and worthy of love. Whoever has only a slight notion of the great importance of a just order of political and economic life for peace and man's capacity for love, cannot honestly claim that he loves his fellowman if he fails to make every effort to achieve justice in private, social and political life. However, he who clings only to the letter of the law and who is out only for services according to the principle of parity, without being mindful of interpersonal love, discredits justice, too; he is not truly just in the Christian sense, that is, he is unable to articulate love and he does not contribute to the love of man.

Love is the principal prerequisite for the virtue of *prudence*; prudence, however, is the eye of love, the concern about the genuine possibilities of dialogue and service, of the encounter between the "I," the "you," and the "we." Prudence is the fine tact of conscience in a concrete situation. He who loves and wants to grow in his love will attempt his best not only to acquire an abstract knowledge of the moral principles, but also a loving knowledge of human nature and conditions of life; he will also endeavor to learn from the experience and wisdom of others. Like love, the Christian virtue of prudence is always in need of growth; that is to say, we are not prudent unless we are ready to learn even from our mistakes and those of our fellowmen. We are on the right road to prudence if we are willing to admit humbly our own imprudence.

Christian love is strong-minded and valiant; it resists unswervingly the temptation of evil, no matter whether it arises from the unexpurgated abyss of a man's own being or whether it approaches us from the world around us. The Christian virtue of *fortitude* is that enduring power of love which does not give in to evil, but which itself overcomes evil in its nonviolent and infinitely powerful attitude of love. The greatest act of bravery is patience and endurance when it is necessary to suffer, so that the kingdom of love might prevail over evil and gentleness over those who make it difficult for us to love. This gentleness and persevering patience is possible only if, in situations of conflict, we are as concerned about the well-being and salvation of those who put us to the test as about self-preservation—preservation of community out of an unshakable love.

Christian love is manifested in the virtue of

gentleness. Confucius ranks it among the four cardinal virtues, or as he says, "among the four most precious gifts which heaven bestows on man." It includes also the constant endeavor to learn from the good habits and manners of others; it is vigilant in its expression. Its actual source and strength is, however, loving kindness, a heart at peace in its unwavering love.

Christian love cannot sing its song if *self-control*, the combined virtues of discipline and temperance, is missing in its chorus. This virtue, however, is possible only for the sons and daughters of Adam if they deny themselves, that is, if they suppress vigilantly a false kind of self-love which would disperse and squander their energies.

Love Fulfills the Commandments

The meaning of the commandments and, above all, of those found in the second table of the Decalogue, is the protection of love. A love which is yet incomplete needs the protection and the warning signals of the commandments. The perfect love in heaven will have no more need for them. Yet it is only a growing love that gradually comes to understand the true meaning of the commandments. They are not an adjunct of love, but stand completely in the service of the love by which and in which man truly finds himself.

The *first three commandments* protect the love of God; the object of the second table is the ordering of love of neighbor, the order of love among men.

The *fourth commandment* stakes out the

realm of the family, the most decisive community of love. In the respectful love for their parents, children honor the love of their parents for each other. This is the fountain of life and an especially powerful source for a good training of mind and body; ultimately children gratefully honor God for the gift of life which has been bestowed on them out of love and with respect to the fulfillment of love.

The *fifth commandment* covers the goods of physical life and the health of the whole person entrusted to men in mutual responsibility. He who is willing to spend his energies and to sacrifice his life together with Christ slowly or suddenly in the service of neighbor and community, will never sin against the health and life of his neighbor. He who lacks love erodes his own life and brings the poisoned drop of bitterness and discord into the life of many others.

Human sexuality reveals its final meaning only in faithfully dedicated love. The *sixth commandment* protects the meaning of this love in which the marriage partners not only assist each other in lovingly perfecting themselves, but also strengthen that upon which depends the future of the human race. In this perspective, the youth keep themselves open to the calling either to marriage or to celibacy.

The *seventh commandment* reminds us that all temporal things, even our personal capabilities, are all gifts of the one heavenly Father with respect to love among His children. Only he who strives to receive everything gratefully as a gift of the love of God and who uses it as a means to express love in the community can truly be just and can truly delight in everything.

The *eighth commandment* protects the love due our neighbor in truth and truth in love. Honesty is to be expressed in our words and deeds if as Christians we are to witness to the truth of salvation.

The *ninth and tenth commandments* remind us that it is impossible to maintain an external order if our hearts and our sentiments are in a state of disorder. They convey the fundamental moral appeal: "Be renewed in your mind."

The Decalogue does not comprise the entire law for a Christian; indeed, he who refuses to do anything beyond the letter of the Decalogue is far from being a true Christian. He also misunderstands the Decalogue, for, according to the intentions of God, it was to serve as a signpost leading us to the Sermon on the Mount, to the law of the new Covenant. Only he whose attention focuses on the growth of love in accordance with the Sermon on the Mount will understand the full meaning of the Decalogue.

Questions for Further Discussion

1. Are the applications the author draws out of the beatitudes in terms of love of neighbor realistic for everyone, at least as goals?

2. Discuss the statement that "we Christians are the only Christ that many people will ever see." Whose responsibility is it if the world does not see Christ in us?

3. What is the primary reason for striving for "perfection"? What is the true meaning of virtue?

4. What does the author mean when he says that the meaning of the Commandments is in their being the "protection of love"?

5. Draw out a practical way of life based on the matter discussed in this chapter.

IV
The Coming of Age of Christian Love

At times, modern man superficially interprets St. Augustine's words: "Be mindful of love and do 'as you please.'" Either he hears only the second part of the sentence, "do as you please," or he fails to realize the tremendous implications contained in the first part of the sentence, "Be mindful of love"—that is, have love.

The understanding of the true meaning of love requires constant effort and study even though such knowledge of Christ and the heavenly Father ultimately remains a gift of faith. Anyone knowing the true meaning of love in every situation ranks far above the most learned of modern scholars and scientists. Yet to possess genuine love—to be a loving person—is infinitely greater. He who fully understands the meaning of love and its requirements will be receptive to its demands and thereby prove himself mature.

Constant Conversion as the Way to Maturity

Man enters the world not only as a minor but as a stranger in a world of adults and children where there is an ongoing struggle between true and unenlightened love, between unselfish concern and exploitation. Our own heart is wavering between the Adamic self-centered man who sees all things in relation to his ego and the redeemed man who is open to God and respectful of the dignity and uniqueness of his neighbor.

We are enriched through our experience of the genuine unselfish love of our parents and friends. At the same time, we are bound to experience the hard realities of life and the disappointment of our own limitations and narrow-mindedness.

Both the positive and negative experiences of our life may be used as raw materials for the building blocks of our own future maturity. In the spirit of faith man discerns God's gracious invitation in every circumstance of his life which invites him to reach a decision. Man makes progress on the road to Christian maturity when he accepts himself and when, in the growing awareness of his abilities and limitations, he gathers his forces to overcome the inclinations and tendencies of his own ego. Genuine acceptance of self presupposes acceptance of others despite their limitations and shortcomings. It implies a humble acceptance and recognition of all the good received from them.

Christian maturity includes the humble acceptance of our very lack of maturity, of our limitations and even our sinfulness. Yet it has nothing in common with a fatalistic attitude or any self-complacency. Maturity is a goal to be sought during a lifetime. At the same time, it is a blueprint outlining not only the chief direction or aim but also indicating the various steps along the path toward an ever more perfect maturity. Aware of our limitations and the burden of past neglects, man must know in what direction he is to grow. The decisive word regarding the way and direction should be Christ's own: "I am the way, the truth, and the life" (John 14:6).

A Christian who has achieved a certain degree of maturity is not beset and confused by the riddles of life, neither does he possess all the answers in the form of clear-cut directives and precepts. He rather places himself in the presence of Christ, opening his heart and mind to listen. He is able to perceive God's call and invitation even if at times it might be obscure. The Christian, who like Christ centers his life around the will and interest of the heavenly Father's will, has truly found direction, strength and personal freedom. On the other hand, the man whose orientation is his own ego, will get lost, confused and paralyzed. Egocentricity makes man unhappy and despondent.

While still on his earthly pilgrimage, man is in need of constant vigilance and effort if he truly wishes to follow Christ. Although man finds his true self-fulfillment in following Christ, he must beware of his arbitrary ego misleading him from his goal-directed striving toward Christ. Vigilance makes man alert to opportunities for good. It also demands that he scrutinize his motives so that his good works may be done in view of Christ whom he truly will see and love in his neighbor; otherwise, man will run the risk of a certain idolatry, of dancing around the golden calf of selfishness.

Christian vigilance derives its strength from a sincere determination to oppose the selfish ego in all its various manifestations, so that man may open himself more and more to the "you" of God and the "we" of neighbor and community. This is basically the meaning of Christian self-denial, mortification or constant conversion.

Two Forms of Personalism

Man's history is characterized by the tension between the image of man as portrayed by Adam and the absolutely mature man represented by Christ Jesus.

Adam and Eve looked away from God, indeed they hid from His sight as soon as they began to worry selfishly about their maturity, their freedom, their wisdom and their self-fulfillment. Eve started her soliloquy with the dark abyss of the selfish self, within which are hidden all the forces of evil. An ego all entangled in itself urges isolation in independence from the "you" of God: "The woman saw that the tree was good to eat and pleasing to the eye, and that it was desirable for the knowledge that it could give; so she took some of its fruit and ate it. Then the eyes of both of them were opened and they realized that they were naked" (Gen. 3:6-7).

Adam's personalism is a personalism which turned away from God. It is characterized not only by the fact that Adam and Eve are hiding from God—since He has become a reason for fear, the fear for self-realization and arbitrary maturity—but also by man's overbearing attitude toward the woman: "It was the woman you put with me; she gave me the fruit" (Gen. 3:12). In this kind of personalism, man will try to lord over woman (Gen. 3:16); he will despise her dignity in polygamy and try to impress her with his audacity and superiority over others (Gen. 4:19-24). A personalist filled with the Adamic desire for a selfish self-fulfillment will associate with the "you" because whatever he does, he does only with reference to his own self-glorification.

His selfishness will prompt him to desert his partner as soon as it appears that she no longer furthers his desire to advance and glorify him.

The Adamic personalist may not always act as obviously as did Lamech, descendant of Cain and heir to the old urban culture: "Hear my voice, Lamech's wives, listen to what I say: I killed a man for wounding me, a boy for striking me" (Gen. 4:23). Such a man can also disguise himself as a moralist who wants to put everything —religion, world and man—into the service of his own self-perfection. Great benefactor that he may be—he might give away all his possessions—but ultimately not for the sake of others, but rather in order to produce the image of a perfect man rich with merits. Perhaps his stoic determination will subdue his passions, including his capacity for joy—and yet he does this, ultimately, out of a concern for the protection of his own ego, in an ever-increasing incapacity to share happiness and sorrow with others. Hidden beneath his cowl, he may dedicate his life to a contempt for the world for the sake of his own "salvation," without really caring for the wholesomeness of either world or fellowman. He will vie with the zealous Pharisee in observing the law's smallest detail in order to seek in the law his own righteousness, not hearing his fellowman's cries for love and charity, unconcerned with honoring God's wish to reveal Himself as the Father of all.

These personalists will not only fill the pages of history; they will build chairs and pulpits for themselves, they will establish their own schools of philosophy and religion. Some will make frequent use of God, others will deny Him with or without vehemence. But common to them all, despite all differences, is the characteristic of considering everything in soliloquy with the superego, with the serpent of selfish righteousness. In self-chosen isolation, forgetful of the presence of God or man, he is concerned only with his personal freedom and status as an adult.

But we probably never will meet such a perfect specimen of this type of frustrated personalist, a self-made god completely entangled in his own self. In the most remote corner of such a man's heart there somehow still remains the call for the "you" that wants to be taken seriously for its own sake. Somewhere one will hear the cry: "What a wretch I am! Who will save me from this isolationary personalism?" "Thanks be to God through Jesus Christ our Lord!" (Rom. 7:24). Christ is the new Adam, the Redeemer of unredeemed personalism, as well as of the disorder of modern mass society.

Christ understands Himself and lives as a person coming from and going to the Father, as the messenger of the Father's love anointed by the Holy Spirit to sacrifice Himself for His brothers for the sake of revealing the love of God. "Christ did not think of himself" (Rom. 15:3). In the Easter mystery the true victory of self is realized in dedication to the "you." And this is not a mere myth: It is a historical event which makes history, indeed gives ultimate meaning to the whole of history.

Through the grace of God, man can look up to Christ in faith and thus understand his own personality as a call from God. By faithfully listening to Christ's call, the ego opens up to the "you" in other human beings with the best of its possibilities. The more intensified our belief in Christ becomes, the more receptive we become to the call for reverential and unselfish—and therefore joyful—love and responsibility to our neighbor in the community. As our belief in Christ progresses and deepens, it brings about a progressive openness toward our fellowman unless it is impeded by special psychological and sociological causes.

Accordingly, the commandment of love is not merely added like an ingredient to the decisive condition of a person: It rather expresses and realizes the ultimate and best possibility of the person created in the image of God. The person develops according to the divine plan; he realizes himself in surrendering himself in faith to Christ, which presupposes and produces openness and service to the "you" and to the "we" of the community. The redeemed person finds his true self in the I-you-we relationship after the example of Christ.

In the complexity of life, as well as in the rational efforts of theologians and philosophers, all kinds of transitions are found between the Adamic person and a personalism that assimilates itself to Christ. We are forever working to overcome the selfish personalism and to fulfill our personality in union with Christ.

Readiness and Ability to Take Responsibility

Loving a person as a person is not merely a matter of instinct or blind passion. It is an answer to the gift and call of a love that centers

around the "you" rather than the "I." Genuine
Christian love and maturity grow with the ability
to listen, with empathy, and the willingness not
to offer a premeditated love to the other human
being, but to respond and to serve him in accordance with his reasonable wishes and his
willingness to listen to us.

The morality of Christian love is not a
pedantic clinging to rules covered with dust, nor
is it a playful confidence in our own good intentions. Of course, good intentions and good
attitudes are a prerequisite for proper orientation, for the ability to listen. But orientation does
not release us from the task of looking intently
to the reality and its structures. Christian ethics
is, indeed, an ethics of attitudes and of responsibility.

But such an ethics requires an intimate knowledge of human nature and of the world; a knowledge of one's own ego in all its heights and
depths; a knowledge of our fellowman and of
our environment; a knowledge of the importance
of customs and of the structures of law; a
knowledge of economy, art and public opinion,
to mention only a few. Our actions are not only
a manifestation of our sentiments; they are also
always an encroachment on our own history and
on the fate of other men. They seep deep into the
"you" and "I," and spread out into the construc-
tion of an external order which sustains man.

Increasing knowledge about the limits of one's
competence, about human nature and the world,
is a decisive step toward maturity. Willingness
to assume responsibility must be measured by the
capacity to bear such responsibility. This is

particularly true of such fundamental decisions as the choice of a marriage partner, taking up a government position, or beginning a career in journalism. A person with a tendency to faint-heartedness and with only a limited knowledge of the psychological facts of life is not acting responsibly if she or he chooses a marriage partner with a marked tendency to get angry very easily or to get drunk.

Man's maturity is a progressive phenomenon; it implies willingness to learn from others, to accept counsel, even to make mistakes . . . as long as one is willing to correct them and to accept the consequences. No man is born either an artist or a scholar; initial failures should not discourage us. Yet it is necessary that we learn early in life to cope with failure. Maturity requires a responsible choice of vocation in view of one's special gifts and talents.

There is a romantic kind of "responsibility ethics" which hardly deserves the name of ethics. It attempts to do away with all rules of social conduct, all the moral laws, thus making the person's solitary decision the sole criterion in a given situation. Even the most gifted man, even the genius stands in need of social rules, of traditional forms of politeness; and in questions of morals, he needs time-honored concepts and the fundamental principles of moral conduct.

The child and the adolescent, particularly, need more than a rational external order. Up to a certain point, they also need the guidance and control of the educator or person in authority. All this should be interpreted as aiming toward a more responsible person. The imperatives must, therefore, not be presented arbitrarily. The yardstick of Christian education and use of authority must not be blind obedience, but insight into a command and above all respect and knowledge of the other person.

Both our pluralistic society and our ever-changing world need the greatest possible number of men who are willing and able to take on responsibility. Otherwise, the society and the world will degenerate into dictatorship and slavish conformity. An attempt to educate with mere imperatives, with laws, rules and statutes, drives the stronger individuals of the younger generation into open rebellion; the danger exists that the weaker ones are being prepared to conform to different attitudes and concepts which these young men and women, who have become unable to act on their own, are bound to confront accidentally at some point in their lives. If 19-year-old Jean, who has learned nothing else at home and in the parish but to be docile and obedient, accidentally runs into gangs, beatniks or rowdies, she very likely will assimilate herself with the same "docility."

Room for Initiative and Freedom

A jet airplane requires quite a long runway. Man, too, needs sufficient room for free initiative—including the possibility of making mistakes. If we are to expect him to grow into a mature and responsible human being, a child or adolescent must have the opportunity to develop his creative talents, particularly in the sphere of morals—that is, in his search for the corresponding expression of genuine charity and

58

responsibility for the "you," for the community and for himself. Therefore, rules and commandments must not be overly strict.

In this regard, a significant correspondence can be noticed between the psychological requirements for a gradual personal maturity, on the one hand, and a shift in emphasis from the "border law" to the "target commandment" in the Sermon on the Mount, on the other. Life in accordance with the Sermon on the Mount, and particularly under the conditions of life in modern society, calls for a Christian who has a highly developed and deep insight into the nature of the good, and who has the psychic energies and the initiative and courage needed to take on responsibility.

Education and personal growth in accordance with this ideal is not free of risks. This ideal cannot possibly be achieved without some mistakes. If, however, one stakes everything on legalistic narrow-mindedness and maximum control in order to avoid some of the risks of a morality of love and responsibility, then one has rescued oneself from the risk of life through the choice of death, through a moral suicide. The proper handling of this dilemma calls for facing the risks and aiming at the golden mean. Christian maturity is a goal which can be approached only gradually, a goal for which one must constantly strive by mobilizing all forms of skill and knowledge. The more Christianity is able to produce truly responsible and mature individuals, the more will she also undertake to guarantee human dignity to persons wanting in the psychological and moral spheres.

Fulfilled Existence

Christian religion and morality should not be used for self-aggrandizement or the search for satisfaction and self-fulfillment. A mature Christian loves the good for its own sake, that is, he is open to the "you" and the "we"; he reciprocates love; he gathers all the energies of love particularly when a fellowman is in danger of succumbing due to lack of charity.

However, it is not wrong to keep one's own fulfillment in mind as long as God and fellowman are not exploited for selfish reasons, but are loved for their own sake. It is part of our confidence in God and the power of love that, in our dedication to the good, we also expect, ultimately, our own personal fulfillment. But this fulfillment must not be confused with a short-term payment, a remuneration, or with self-satisfaction. The good by its nature is equipped with the power to make us happy; yet, it cannot give complete happiness so long as we selfishly search for our ego in our charitable endeavors.

Questions for Further Discussion

1. In the light of the discussion in this chapter, what is true maturity?

2. What does it mean to take Christ as "the way, the truth, and the life"? How does this help us to maturity?

3. Distinguish between the personalism of Adam and that of Christ. Does a discussion on this matter have any bearing on your own personal life?

4. Try to describe some cases of mistaken "personalism."

5. What does one have to do to increase one's ability to take responsibility?

6. Discuss the "risk-taking" involved in living a life in accord with the Sermon on the Mount particularly in modern society.

V

The Person in Community and Society

The first general councils of the Church were characterized by their struggle for an adequate expression of the mystery of the Blessed Trinity, particularly the true humanity and divinity of Christ. Today's questions center around man, the human person and the community. If we ask our questions without turning to the mystery of the Divine Persons, then our concern for man can easily lead us into fallacies, even those of atheism. "Some extol man so extravagantly that their faith in God becomes anemic, though they seem more inclined to affirm man than to deny God" (*Pastoral Constitution on the Church in the Modern World*, Art. 19).

In modern philosophy, a personalistic approach predominates. It finds its adherents among all kinds of people, because it corresponds to modern man's basic experiences, to his fears and hopes. Our present generation has seen unscrupulous dictatorships trample human dignity underfoot and turn man into an object of cold-blooded calculation. Mao Tse-tung is joining the ranks of Hitler and Stalin when he asserts that in the case of a war the loss of 100 or 200 million men would not mean much to China.

Human dignity and man's capacity for love are further endangered by a highly structured and impersonal society. A worker who spends eight hours a day on a deadening assembly line, or at other depersonalizing types of work, deeply appreciates the personal relationships in family, marriage, courtship and friendship. Man desires to be more than a mere wheel in a machine, more than a useful member of a functional community. Man, considered only in view of his contribution or used as a mere commodity, feels alienated, threatened and lost. He wants to be recognized and appreciated as a person.

Community With God and Earthly Community

The *Pastoral Constitution on the Church in the Modern World,* in its structure and reasoning, states this expectation of modern man clearly: "Above all the Church knows that her message is in harmony with the most secret desires of the human heart when she champions the dignity of the human vocation, restoring hope to those who have already despaired of anything higher than their present lot. Far from diminishing man, her message brings to his development light, life and freedom" (*Pastoral Constitution on the Church in the Modern World,* Art. 21).

The decisive aspect in the Church's message remains always the personal communion of man with God: Man is a person, because God calls him personally and because God makes him capable of responding in love. Man fully realizes himself as a person through his acts of love, and a faith inspired by love—a faith which becomes active in fraternal love. Christian morality must seriously involve itself with the full realization of the human community and the earthly society in order to strengthen the genuineness of faith and of personal encounter with God. Not only does faith demand the attitude and act of love, but in many respects, it also builds on human experience in community and society. A genuine communion of love prepares the way for a vital and joyful belief in the God of love.

The man whose experiences are limited to those of a community or society geared and oriented toward selfish goals will likewise tend to envision God in a purely utilitarian way. He will run the risk of seeing Him in the role of a large-scale manager. Such a man will use the sacraments as means and make use of indulgences and religious services with petty calculations toward his own security. His religious vocabulary becomes characterized by utilitarian categories of "means and end." Such an impoverished approach is responsible for producing the priest who acts like a career man and thereby becomes a deterrent of good and a source of unbelief for many.

The father of Karl Marx followed the example of many citizens when he decided to have himself and his entire family baptized in order to promote his business, thereby implanting contempt for religion in the heart of the young Marx. He hated religion which was, on the one hand, a sentimental veil over the stark realities of life, and on the other, a means for worldly gain. His experience in his immediate community barred him from understanding the true meaning of religion as a brotherhood or a community centered around the all-holy and all-loving God.

A petty, despotic and forever nagging father on the one hand, and an intimidated mother on the other, can give rise to an utterly wrong idea of God: The image of their father can influence children throughout their lives in regard to their prayer, their confession and their contempt of religion, often manifesting itself in an obsessive-compulsive neurosis or an ultimate denial of God.

God is not a product of human fancy. He is Our Lord and Creator, whether we recognize Him or not. But the mode of our religious openness, our receptivity, our confidence, our gratitude, even of our visual disturbances, and our isolation, depends largely on our experiences in the family community and larger society. This is a cogent reason why we should make every possible effort for well-structured earthly communities. Marriage and the family should be our primary social concern, but not the only one.

Family, Society and State

In our daily lives as well as in literature and philosophy, we frequently encounter a type of "personalism" which concerns itself only with the immediate personal relationships in marriage, family and friendship while either completely ignoring society and state or merely accepting them passively or as necessary evils. A similar attitude can be seen with regard to one's vocation and career—they are considered only as a means of livelihood, necessary to raise a family. The proper perspective and relationship between the fundamental personal communities and the social and political life is of prime importance for the future of mankind, for the full development of the person and, last but not least, for the mission of Christians in the world.

The Church will not cease to teach and stress

the fact that the family is the fundamental community, where man can and should learn the true meaning of love and the spirit of responsibility. Here we encounter one of the insurmountable contradictions between the Christian and the classical Marxist view. In Marxism, modern man is a social being. The end and meaning of education is the Marxist economic society. Since 1956, roughly seven million children in the Soviet Union were systematically raised in the "factory of the new Soviet man" according to the highly effective psychological methods of the leading Communist social psychologist, A. S. Makarenko. As early as the age of three months, the little ones are exposed to "collective education." From the collective nursery school to the university, everything is aimed toward discipline and efficiency of the Soviet citizen. The results are, as the experts tell us, very good: Already at the age of 18 months these children can eat and dress all by themselves and are even toilet trained. At a very early age, they join the group and teach one another; they even criticize one another. In view of their efficiency, their social adaptation, and obedience these children are undoubtedly normal, indeed, frequently better developed than those who grow up within their families. But their emotional life is characterized by a striking deprivation and dependency. It seems that the Red Guards, who are such a pliable tool in the hands of Mao, likewise received such a kind of education.

Granted that here and there we could learn quite a bit from the psychology of Makarenko, we must nevertheless clearly understand that we cannot aspire to this kind of success. In our view, the great success is not the conformist or the robot, but the man who is capable of love and who lives according to a personal conscience oriented toward and responsive to the fundamental value of love. In that light, the family is normally irreplaceable. There the children learn above all a respect for the "you," a spontaneous and, at the same time, disciplined love. Our best Christian orphanages and reform schools for broken-up families are guided by this philosophy: The children are brought up in groups which imitate the natural conditions of the family as closely as possible.

On the other hand, the social teachings of the Church do not overlook the fact that the family must be responsive to social and political responsibility. Personalism, in the Christian sense, certainly does not mean isolation within the intimate community of the family, but rather a humanization of all the spheres of life in the spirit of love and respect, initiative and responsibility, freedom and obedience. These are best learned in the well-ordered atmosphere of a family.

Often enough modern sociology has documented the interaction between family and society, family and culture, family and economy, and family and career. The family as an institution can be healthy only to the extent that families are aware of their responsibility for the right organization of culture, economy, society and the political order. Conversely, culture, society and state can truly prosper and remain human only when they consider themselves coresponsible for a healthy development of family life.

Man is a unified whole; every attempt to break

up his life into a personal and an impersonal sphere destroys the unity of man. This was also acknowledged to some extent by Makarenko, even more so than by the many Communists who apply his methods. He emphasizes that parents and teachers figure prominently in man's development. Man enters into a variety of personal and social relationships. If we want to become the "salt of the earth," we must clearly understand the influences for good and evil in the world around us, particularly the effects of evil influences. We must work with others to imprint on our world the stamp of love and responsibility, the stamp of genuine humanity.

Personalism on Different Levels

Primitive animism not only sees life and spirit in everything; it is also unable to see the difference between persons, animals and things. Those who believe in the migration of the soul would rather let their brothers starve than assent to the killing of the traditionally holy cows, while a Christian personalist distinguishes clearly between a person or a community of persons on the one hand, and things, factual processes, biological functions and organisms on the other. This does not mean that he is not affected by those things which are not directly an expression of the human person. The love of the Creator and of many men, of entire generations, or the lack of love or responsibility on the part of man, finds expression in everything.

It is the task of the human person to understand—particularly in man but also in everything else—the language of God, the divine spark of the Creator's power, and to use everything in such a way that beyond its temporary usefulness, it also expresses humaneness, justice, goodness, reverence and responsibility. A few examples might shed some light on what we have said so far.

A well-cultivated home, be it poor or rich, is more than a mere shelter against the weather; it is not only highly useful economically, but it has affective values, also. It radiates a certain spiritual climate. A home is made comfortable and attractive by the love of those who live in it. The flowers on the table, selected with the husband's taste in mind, are part of the loving reception he meets when he returns from work or from a trip.

A family dinner is more than the feeding of hungry people; it embodies the father's work, the mother's loving care, a feeling of togetherness and tender consideration. The careful preparation of food finds its full response not only in a hearty appetite, but also in the gratitude, the recognition, the consideration for the thoughts and attitudes expressed in it.

A dinner at a hotel may be expensive and superbly prepared; nevertheless, it does not possess the same personal values of a modest meal prepared by a loving wife or mother. This does not mean that we should not think gratefully of those people who serve us and who prepare our meals at the hotel. A friendly and sincere expression of gratitude to the persons waiting on us is part of the humaneness of the meal and of our truly human behavior, even though it does not take on the intimate level of a family meal.

A conversation between engaged or married people is something entirely different from the factual discourse with our employer or the teller who cashes our check. Even though we are on a different level here, we must not forget for a single moment that we are dealing with human beings. A friendly greeting creates an atmosphere of love and respect. An employee in an office or a department store may be unfriendly and peevish today because she does not feel well or because she has been offended by her fiancé or her husband; if my reaction is unfriendly and arrogant, I merely aggravate her problem without being aware of it. However, if I find a word of kindness or have a sense of humor, then perhaps I might even turn into a peacemaker.

But touching the right note or finding the right word is not enough. We Christians are personalists when we treat our employer and our co-workers justly, and when we perform our work with a feeling of responsibility to all the other persons connected with the business. However, if we do our work only in view of the salary or for the sake of our career, we are not Christian personalists in the proper sense of the word, but rather impersonal individualists.

The political arena is not a family affair, nor is it a sports club; the language spoken there is considerably different from that used among classmates or art buffs. Even in the heat of an argument with a political opponent, however, the Christian personalist will never forget that his opponent is a person with the right to respect and a good name. A nobility which conveys to the neighbor our belief in the honesty of his intentions—either implicit or explicit—contributes to the humanizing of politics and is superior to an objective argument. In addition, a Christian personalist will not forget for a single moment that both in politics and in daily life the well-being of every human person is at stake, not only the mere prestige of a selected few or the power of factions.

A political argument is in many respects different from an argument among theologians or a dialogue between confessor and penitent. Anyone who tries to carry through all three kinds of conversation on the same level would miss the point. During an argument between theologians it is a matter of the best possible recognition of the truth that God revealed; therefore, it is not enough that theologians say niceties to each other where the truth of salvation may be at stake. But if they turn a theological argument into a personal weapon or an attack against schools of the Church, they betray both truth and personalism. Only when they listen to each other in a spirit of love, when they make an honest effort to understand each other and to express fragmentary insights as humbly and as understandably as possible, only when both partners address each other in the face of God, do they achieve the level proper to them. During confession the dialogue is not a cross-examination, nor a theological lecture, but rather joint praise of God's justice and mercy, a reverent search for the next step on the road to salvation and holiness.

The confessor, the theologian and the politician may be forced to discuss the same subject —for instance, the indissolubility of marriage— but each will discuss it with a different vocabulary and on a different level. The confessor may show a wife who firmly believes in the indissolubility of marriage, but who refuses to resume a normal marital life with her husband, that she is practically forcing her husband into divorcing her; he will relate God's forgiveness to her husband's infidelity and thereby point out to her the only possible solution, namely, to prove her faithfulness by forgiveness. Such a conversation certainly requires the very special atmosphere of prayer, reverence and compassion.

The theologians will resort to every method offered by historical research and, conscious of the various theological criteria, they will discuss how fundamental faithfulness—faithfulness to the principle of the indissolubility of marriage—might be combined with pastoral benevolence when dealing with people who got into a tricky situation through no fault of their own, or even through their own fault.

The politician, on the other hand, will neither talk like a confessor nor preach like a theologian, but, knowing the mentality and the web of political forces, he will search for the arguments and suggestions that, in our modern world, are apt to contribute to the protection of the stability of marriage and the well-being of the innocent partner and children. He, too, acts like a true personalist: He tries to figure out the thinking of his partners and opponents in order to be able to understand their point of view and to convince them, if necessary, of his own ideas. In addition, he will have not only a hazy idea about the common good, but he will envision the welfare of all persons under the law. If he advocates a good piece of family legislation, he knows that he serves not only the abstract idea of the state, but indeed, the living state in view of the best possible well-being of all of its citizens.

The Community of Nations

Jesus replied to the lawyer who asked Him "Who is my neighbor?" by telling the parable of the Good Samaritan who was moved with compassion when he came upon the Jew who fell into the hands of brigands (Luke 10:29-37). This was definitely a shock to the Jews, who would not even speak to a Samaritan—especially since the Lord introduced a person from the other side of the fence as showing compassion. Every man can be my neighbor when Divine Providence leads us together and enables us to do good to each other. We all belong to the great family of God. Christ has sacrificed Himself for everybody. As the redeemed we are called to open ourselves to all men as best we can.

Yet, it would be oversimplifying the idea of personalism if we talked about it only in connection with person-to-person relationships. Considering the steadily increasing social relationships in their ever-growing importance for personal and family life, a Christian personalist will devote himself to the cultivation of good international relations on all possible levels. The breadth of Catholic thinking and believing must be reflected in a willingness to accept worldwide responsibility. No one can honestly claim "I believe in the one Catholic Church" unless he identifies himself with the unity of Christianity and of nations within the limits of his position and competence.

The reasons inciting a Christian personalist to become a patriot for the progress and welfare of his fatherland will also compel him to do everything in his power to further the community of nations, the peace on earth, just international agreements, and an end to hunger in the world through the promotion of developing nations. No Christian can bypass this perspective, especially after the encyclicals *Mater et Magistra* and *Pacem in Terris* of Pope John, the peace efforts of Pope Paul, the *Pastoral Constitution on the Church in the Modern World* of the Second Vatican Council, as well as several similar resolutions drawn up by the World Council of Churches. This is the proper way of speaking of God, the Creator and Redeemer of all mankind.

Questions for Further Discussion

1. Why must Christian morality seriously concern itself with realizing the human community and the earthly society? Contrast this stress with the "otherworldly" spirituality of the recent past.

2. Discuss the many ways in which a person can "use" religion for his own selfish purposes.

3. What is the difference between what the author calls the Marxist view of man and the Christian one?

4. What is a Christian personalist?

5. How would you answer the question "Who is my neighbor?"

VI
We Are the Church

Many have suffered because of the Church, and indeed, have not known what to make of her. The working class and, generally, the lowest social strata could never understand the showy titles and language of a "higher" clergy that affiliated itself with the higher social classes. The last century brought on the greatest emigration that ever occurred in the history of the Church. One spoke of the Church as dying in men's souls before there was any mention of God's absence from their lives.

There are certainly various reasons for this phenomenon. Pope John and the Council caused the world to take a renewed interest in the Church, an interest unheard of previously. New hopes flared. The bishops gathered for the Council and professed a program of renewal in humility, in obedience to the Gospels and in docility to the Holy Spirit in accordance with the all-encompassing commandment of love. In spite of initial tensions, a surprisingly broad agreement was reached in the final votes on the models to the various constitutions. After all, what did those 75 votes "not in favor" mean when compared to the 2,309 votes "in favor" (December 7, 1965) when the longest and most daring document of the Council was put to the vote? Except for the members of the *Comitato Romano* (an organized group of conservative bishops) everybody held high hopes that the ship of the Church was on her course to new horizons.

Meanwhile, the signs indicate that the ship of Peter will still encounter stormy days, less because of enemies from without than because of tensions that must be resolved from within. Many observed, with fear and distrust, all the apparent or actual attempts made by a small but powerful conciliar opposition to prove that the Council had met with failure after all. Militant groups of traditionalists organized themselves.

Progressive groups now interpret the helplessness or hesitation of bishops or Church authorities as a secret or open conspiracy with the fanatic traditionalists, a suspicion which, by and large, lacks any foundation. In this climate of distrust, the radicalism of many a "reformer" mushrooms. Eloquent laymen and priests raise impatient voices in the name of a passionate interest in and love of the Church.

And while the aged Maritain is ostracizing extremists of the Left and prophets of a thorough reform, in a mixture of humor and irony, Charles Davis, a hitherto quiet and circumspect theologian with the highest reputation in the English-speaking world, appears on TV and declares to the world his decision to leave the Church he finds unloving and corrupt. His starting signal for a "better" Christianity without the Church is— aside from vague charges against the entire Church—a special, far-from-loving incrimination of the pope.

Only God can pass the final judgment here; He alone knows the entire tragedy of this and many other cases of mistaken people in the Church. The extremists in the reactionary camp certainly have no reason to rejoice, if they are concerned about the Church and not only about proving that they were right all along when they prophesied that "Fifty years would not be enough to rectify all the mistakes of Pope John."

If we love the Church—and we cannot truly love Christ, the Lord of the Church, unless we love His Church—then we have every reason to ponder our own role. Would Charles Davis ever have been able to pass a judgment so summary, so harsh, so unloving and unjust, if he had first examined himself, in everything he suffered because of the Church, according to the principle: We all are the Church? If we begin, like outsiders, to stare constantly at the few dozens of officials of the Church who have turned apathetic, and if, by looking at them, we take offense at the entire Church, then we have forgotten that we are ourselves a part of the Church; more, we are blindly overlooking the many devoted bishops and priests and all the many genuine Christians.

Christ's Suffering Because of Us— Because of His Church

There is an unchristian way to cope with the imperfections and sins in the Church—we dismiss everything with the remark: "Oh well, they are human like everybody else. Why should they be any different?" Even an Alexander VI and his son, Cesare Borgia, born out of wedlock, are accepted, for "they were products of their time." We are annoyed with senile prelates who desperately try to hold on to their offices chiefly because such conduct is no longer fashionable in our modern, business-oriented society.

This attitude is no less a betrayal of the

Church than the anguished cry of Charles Davis. Christ has suffered because of the temporal thinking of His Apostles and disciples. He spoke harshly to Peter who dared try to talk Him out of His desire to suffer and die for His people (Matt. 16: 21-23), and who was so sure of himself when he declared that he would not lose faith even when all the others might (Matt. 26:33-35). His sleepy Apostles were a special source of suffering to the Lord on the Mount of Olives.

If we believe in the mystery of the Church and then see how traditionalists keep systematically aloof, concerning themselves only with their own ideas and fighting each other in full view of the Pentecostal storm of the Second Vatican Council, then this must be a source of deep suffering to us. But we must not scream with fear as if the Lord were no longer present on the ship. We must not overlook all the good aspects of the Church, her openness in order, her order in openness, her honest search and scrutiny, and the holy lives of so many simple believers, religious, priests and bishops.

If we believe that the entire people of God is called to sanctity, we will not merely accuse prelates and theologians, but above all, we will feel the pangs of our own contribution and humbly confess our own failures.

We Are the Church of Sinners

The overly zealous servants who wanted to weed out the darnel sprouting with the new wheat would have thoroughly trampled down the field and all the seed with it. They are not only like those priests who, in their relentless rigorism—

particularly in matters which are not part of the unchanging laws of God—have driven many out of the Church or, indeed, have barred them from receiving the sacraments; they are also like those impatient theologians and laymen who, in their zeal for reform, are pulling the authority of the Church to pieces.

If Our Lord were faced with the bitter criticism of bishops and priests who seem either too flexible or too narrow-minded, would He not call these modern executioners to account by saying, "If there is one of you has not sinned, let him be the first to throw a stone" (John 8:8)?

In an age like ours, criticism cannot be avoided. But criticism can serve as a cleanser, as a basis for building, only when it is inspired by love and uttered in a spirit of humility. Even when controversies and criticisms arise—criticisms of certain attitudes and opinions which, in our way of thinking, are wrong and even dangerous—we must not forget that we all expect our salvation from God's mercy only. Those who are eager to hasten the eschatological separation of the "sheep from the goats," and who do not hesitate to count others among the goats and themselves among the sheep, must face the worst final disappointment.

But in this time of transition we must be able to judge for ourselves whose example we ought to follow, and whose word we may heed. We must listen to both warnings of the Sermon on the Mount: "Do not judge, and you will not be judged; because the judgments you give are the judgments you will get" (Matt. 7:1-2) and "Beware of false prophets. . . . You will be able to tell them by their fruits" (Matt. 7:15-16).

We may always hope that failures and/or errors that seem obvious to us are not serious— or, at least, not so serious in God's eyes as man might think. But it is only prudent and in accordance with the Church's teachings for us to be somewhat suspicious and critical of a prelate who, at the Council, fought against the very points which the world's bishops and the successor to Peter taught and promulgated in almost any question, and who then continues to criticize the Council instead of himself, and who declares that nobody should expect him to "change anything which has to do with the way he is and has to be in obedience to the will of God."

A bishop is the official announcer of the Gospel in his diocese and he is the servant of unity; but if he seeks to prevent his priests from applying the Good News of active love to the poor and the victims of discrimination, if he opposes other matters that obviously contradict his service to his colleagues and to unity, then all Christians must be firmly determined to force him to correct his errors. Here it is that mature Christians are tested on their ability to combine humility with firmness and respect with criticism in their discernment of spirits.

If we criticize those who confuse authoritarian conduct with Christ's mission and prejudiced personal opinions with His Gospel, then we must search own own egos just as thoroughly, asking whether we ourselves have not indulged openly or secretly in such temptations. All our criticism is destructive unless we first feel our own contrition, being conscious at every instant that we belong to the Church of sinners and that we take part in the Church's calling to sanctity according to the degree of our humility.

The Teaching Church and the Listening Church

The Church both "upholds the truth and keeps it safe" (I Tim. 3:15). Particularly at a time when everything is in a state of change, we can feel how helpless we would be, in many questions concerning life, if the Church were not our spiritual guide. Christ never ceases to announce the Good News to us and to teach us the truth of salvation through the services of the Church. Christ, who ascended into heaven, pervades the Church with His presence. He bestows on her the promised Spirit of truth; He is the teacher of all men.

All the members of the Church, from the pope down to the child who listened to Jesus' message on his mother's lap, are above all part of the "listening Church"; they are listeners to the Word of God. The Church's teachership is entirely founded on docility. A certain person becomes an authentic teacher in the fullest sense of the word not by holding an office in the Church, but rather by being docile to the utmost, that is, docile to all the different forms through which God teaches us: through Holy Scripture, through the living tradition of the Church, through study of the great theologians, through listening to the wisdom of the humble and the insignificant, through esteem for the religiousness of simple people and of the educated, through attention to the signs of the age, through the example of saints and the virtues of anonymous Christians—and, indeed, of

81

unbelievers—through such scientific achievements of our time as historical research, psychology and sociology.

Genuine docility is to be learned on one's knees, in prayer and confidence in God's grace. Everyone should learn from everyone else, and according to God's way of acting in others. "Each one of us, however, has been given his own share of grace, given as Christ allotted it. . . . And to some, his gift was that they should be apostles; to some, prophets; to some, evangelists; to some, pastors and teachers; so that the saints together make a unity in the work of service, building up the body of Christ. In this way we are all to come to unity in our faith and in our knowledge of the Son of God, until we become the perfect Man, fully mature with the fullness of Christ himself" (Eph. 4:7-13). In these words of St. Paul, the invaluable gift which the magisterium of the Church represents to us becomes discernible. At the same time, it is obviously wrong to split up the Church into a teaching and a learning Church.

To be sure, we are not all the "teaching Church." But we all contribute, either for richness or for impoverishment, in the recognition of truth.

The pope is the supreme teacher of the Church. We owe him special obedience and gratitude. The entire Church must pray to the Holy Spirit for his enlightenment and strength. This does not mean, however, that the pope is not expected to show the highest degree of openness and docility. He is assisted by the Holy Spirit in a very special way, particularly in the few historical moments of a solemn proclamation of a universally binding article of faith; but he does not receive the word directly from the Holy Spirit. That is why the fruitfulness of papal authority is all the greater the more the pope can properly share in the wisdom and experience of the entire assembly of bishops, in the knowledgeability of theologians of all schools of thought, in the experience of laymen from many fields and cultures. The popes somehow have always been the "learning" Church, a fact which was painfully obvious when only a few men with a certain fixed way of thinking were the popes' counselors.

The bishops' teaching authority increases as a function of their docility to the Holy Spirit, exploring every possibility to participate in the fullness of the Church, in all forms of collegiality, in all directions.

The pope teaches with the charism of infallibility only in very unusual moments. Though we owe special docility to his entire activity as the teacher of Christianity, it would be unfair to the uniqueness of the act of faith that the faithful be expected to believe and accept every single utterance of a pope as final and irreformable. We are expected to "acknowledge with reverence and adhere sincerely to the judgments made by him according to his manifest mind and will" (*Constitution on the Church*, Art. 25).

A thorough examination of the documents of the First and Second Vatican Councils permits the theological opinion that the pope is not infallible in questions of mere natural law unless an added aspect of the truth of supernatural revelation is involved. "This infallibility with which the divine Redeemer willed His Church to be endowed in defining a doctrine of faith and morals extends as far as the deposit of divine revelation, which must be religiously guarded and faithfully expounded" (*Constitution on the Church*, Art. 25).

In my opinion, for instance, the encyclical *Casti Connubii* of Pope Pius XI is not a document that can claim infallibility and irreformable finality. This, however, does not mean that we may simply ignore this encyclical. It contains articles of doctrine that cannot be questioned by anyone without giving full license to dangerous errors; for instance, the reference to Matrimony as a divine institution, and the relation of married love to the dignified continuation of life, the dignity of the marital act, the inviolability of unborn life, the absolute obligation to faithfulness because of the marriage bond. Furthermore, the duty and right of the Church as teacher—and particularly of the pope—to guard and recognize these principles must be beyond any doubt.

Discussions presently going on among theologians and the laity concern questions of the application of those principles to a situation that is entirely new in many respects. It is a matter of working out formulations which take into account the novelty of the circumstances and the progress in the various branches of science. If progression without discontinuity is expressed in proper understanding today, this is mainly due to the sometimes heroic obedience of numerous couples to the teachings of *Casti Connubii* and to the honest, humble efforts of theologians to expound loyally the same teachings in the light of the whole of tradition and with a view to the needs and dangers of marriage in our modern age.

Infallibility in every possible question is by no means a necessary prerequisite of authority and obedience. Parents never possess the charism of infallibility and yet they have authority. To be sure, the extent of authority depends on the degree of their maturity, their understanding and humility. The Church does not need to be infallible in matters of natural morality so long as morality is not at odds with divine revelation. In questions of salvation and human wholesomeness, we are sufficiently protected and enlightened, if in matters of natural law, the Church gives us directions which exhaust the present possibilities of knowledge without contradicting divine revelation.

The entire people of God—pope, bishops, priests and laity—must, however, remain continually open to a deeper understanding of revelation, to the unfolding of dogmas and particularly to a deeper understanding of those aspects of moral law which are accessible to reason (natural law).

At a time when humanity is confronted with so many new insights, developments and revolutionary changes, new tasks arise particularly for theology and for the proclamation of the truth of faith and natural morality. To avoid the issue and merely repeat what has been traditionally recognized would mean to betray the Gospel and to epitomize the bad news of "God is dead." The venture of a searching theology forever new, can be carried on successfully only in prayer, in solidarity with the entire people of God and in reverent obedience to the authority of the successors to the Apostles. I often wonder, however, why we do not pray more often for the theologians; criticism is not enough.

The Second Vatican Council has scrutinized these problems with the vigor peculiar to it, above all in its pastoral constitution on the Church: "From the beginning of her history, she has learned to express the message of Christ with the help of the ideas and terminology of various peoples, and has tried to clarify it with the wisdom of philosophers, too. Her purpose has been to adapt the Gospel to the grasp of all as well as to the needs of the learned insofar as such was appropriate. Indeed, this accommodated preaching of the revealed Word ought to remain the law of all evangelization. For thus each nation develops the ability to express Christ's message in its own way. At the same time, a living exchange is fostered between the Church and the diverse cultures of people. To promote such an exchange, the Church requires special help, particularly in our day, when things are changing very rapidly and the ways of thinking are exceedingly various. She must rely on those who live in the world, are versed in different institutions and specialties, and grasp their innermost significance in the eyes of both believers and unbelievers. With the help of the Holy Spirit, it is the task of the entire people of God, especially pastors and theologians, to hear, distinguish, interpret the many voices of our age, and to judge them in the light of the divine Word. In this way, revealed truth can always be more deeply penetrated, better understood, and set forth to greater advantage" (*Constitution on the Church in the Modern World*, Art. 44).

The Sacrament of Love and Unity

The Church's great mission and Christ's prayer for it are the same: "May they all be one. Father, may they be one in us, as you are in me and I am in you, so that the world may believe it was you who sent me" (John 17:21). The community of disciples can be the "salt of the earth" and the "light of the world" only to the extent of their striving humbly and repentantly for unity. "By her relationship with Christ, the Church is a kind of sacrament or sign of intimate union with God, and of the unity of all mankind. She is also an instrument for the achievement of such union and unity" (*Constitution on the Church*, Art. 1).

A sacrament is intelligible and, thus, a sign calling on faith and conscience. When the sacramental sign, the sacramental message, is distorted or falsified into its opposite, we do not have a genuine sacrament anymore; it is no longer an instrument of salvation. Wherever the Church fulfills truth in a spirit of love, she helps to draw men closer to God and to lead them to a greater unity and love of one another. But when "truth" is used as a weapon against one another, or when, because of personal ambition, it is used as a career tool to kindle dissension or indulge in group egoism, there the "sacrament" of Satan is at work.

Christian communities which feel quite comfortable as separate brothers in their separate "homes," who mock one another and are not willing to cooperate for the benefit of suffering mankind, do not live the "sacrament of unity." By engaging in such behavior, they refuse to be intelligible signs of unity.

It is the purpose of the Church's laws to protect her unity and openness to the signs of the times, her mission as an intelligible sign of unity. Anyone who insists on clinging to habits or legal regulations after they have ceased to be a protection of vigilant love and a sign and testimony for the Living God of love stymies the Church's true effectiveness.

On the other hand, anyone who, in the midst of the tensions and anxieties of our times, does everything in his power to strengthen loving unity in truth and genuine unity in love, or who reinstates them, is truly the Church.

Questions for Further Discussion

1. What difference would it make in your own personal attitude toward the Church today if you really realized what it means "to be the Church"?

2. Describe what you think is the right attitude to take toward abuses in the Church and what should be done about them. What is the correct spirit and form for criticism?

3. How does the author describe how one becomes an "authentic teacher" in the Church?

4. What are the benefits and limits of papal infallibility? Why does the author say that infallibility in every question is not a necessary requirement for authority and obedience?

5. Describe the Church as the "sacrament of unity." How did Vatican II help to formulate a plan for the Church to become a true "sign" of God's favor to the world today?

VII
The Christian in Marriage and Family

The family is the prototype and smallest unit of the Church. The Church on earth and the "heavenly Jerusalem" are both referred to as the "family of God." The family is the place where religion and life are either integrated or condemned to hopeless separation.

One of the greatest dangers of our age is precisely this cleavage between religion and life; as a result, religion and morality, too, are on the decline. The sad news that "God is dying" in the souls of men is preceded by a moralism which loosely runs parallel to religion and a certain piety which retreats more and more from actual life. A renewed vigor of religion in the hearts of men has its mainspring in the Christian family, which is conscious of its leading role in the social and religious spheres.

The Meaning of the Sacrament of Matrimony

At times, canonists and moralists have spoken about the sacrament of Matrimony in a way that built a wall between modern man's understanding of marriage and its description in canon law. Such an error also leads to a misunderstanding of marriage in relation to God's will. Many held the opinion that the valid marriage contract itself, as such, constituted the sacrament and, in a one-sided fashion, emphasized the juridical aspects of a valid "contract." All the obligations and purposes of marriage were enumerated, and it was declared that the contract, since it was a sacrament, bestowed grace of itself (*ex opere operato*) so that married people are able to fulfill their duties.

Among the obligations stressed was the requirement that partners in a marriage love each other in a "supernatural way"; thereby conjugal love was considered merely incidental, but not the essential end of marriage. On the other hand, the reaction among both Catholics and Protestants is a denial of this kind of sacramentality of marriage.

Faithful to Holy Scripture and the best of Catholic tradition, the Second Vatican Council offers a much more realistic view of the sacrament of Matrimony. The Council text that concerns itself with the holiness of marriage and of the family characteristically begins with the words: "The intimate partnership of married life and love" (*Pastoral Constitution on the Church in the Modern World,* Art. 48). The word contract is purposely omitted. The bond of marriage is discussed as a *covenant* of irrevocable personal consent. It is not a matter of an impersonal nature relating to duties and law, but rather an indissoluble covenant between two persons, a covenant originating in a free act and which, in its essence, is love in the reciprocal giving of the spouses.

The grace of marriage is not merely God's assistance in the duties and obligations; it is a gift of the powerful works of God's love. It is the special grace of marriage that God calls two human beings to the mutual gift of love and that He makes them capable of loving each other truly and with an ever-greater maturity in their role as parents. The grace of marriage is a gift of God's love, and therefore a calling to genuine love. It is "activated" and becomes fruitful only to the extent that the partner truly reciprocates in love and thus helps the other to a greater love and fidelity. Grace is finally absent in a marriage where the husband and wife fail to work together in order to increase their love, because the specific grace of their vocation has not met with their response.

The meaning of sacrament is: God's saving presence and healing love. The sincerity of the partner's mutual and ever-increasing love and devotion draws Christ's powerful presence. According to the measure of their love they experience this salvific presence.

By virtue of the sincerity of their mutual love they are united in the name of Christ, the Redeemer. "Christ the Lord abundantly blessed this many-faceted love, welling up as it does from the fountain of divine love and structured as it is on the model of His union with the Church. For as the God of old made Himself present to His people through a covenant of love and fidelity, so now the Saviour of men and the Spouse of the Church comes into the lives of married Christians through the sacrament of Matrimony. He abides with them thereafter so that, just as He loved the Church and handed Himself over on her behalf, the spouses may love each other with perpetual fidelity through mutual self-bestowal" (*Pastoral Constitution on the Church in the Modern World,* Art. 48).

It is the special grace and mission of the sacrament of Matrimony that the spouses, through their mutual love, prepare each other for a more meaningful and vital experience of God's love and a more effective love of neighbor. In the first place, the spouses are called upon to love each other deeply and steadfastly; then they will become increasingly able to love their children and to rear them. They will realize: "How rewarding and great must God's love be if man already finds such joy in love! How patient is God's love, because we already manage to be patient, understanding and forgiving!" Grace bears fruit as soon as married people sense the infinite greatness of God's love for their children, when they strive ceaselessly to deepen this experience through their own love. Each mission implies a special grace. Each command and mission presupposes the respective grace to carry out God's design. In Matrimony, the one great commandment —yet more than a commandment in the restricted sense—is that of love. It is a commandment to the extent that we have received and continue to receive more love, the more gratefully we reciprocate it.

Married Love Is Not a Secondary End

The emphasis which the Council and contemporary theology place on conjugal love is, essentially, as old as divine revelation. Man and woman are made for each other so that—both together and individually—they are an image of God, capable of love. The Bible particularly illustrates this in a parable as intelligible to primitive men as to those familiar with modern depth psychology. Eve is created from Adam's rib—that is, she is his true reflection and corresponds to the innermost desires of his heart. Adam rejoices, therefore, at the sight of the gift which God bestowed on him in woman: "This at last is bone from my bones, and flesh from my flesh! This is to be called woman, for this was taken from man. This is why a man leaves his father and mother and joins himself to his wife, and they become one body" (Gen. 2:23-24).

God compares His love for His people with a husband's love for his wife. The Song of Songs, an account of most intimate love between bride and bridegroom, is a song of conjugal love and a praise of God's love. The Council of Trent sums up the essence of traditional thinking on Matrimony when it teaches that "Christ Himself, who instituted the holy sacraments and brought them to perfection, merited for us by His Passion the grace that brings natural love to perfection and strengthens the indissoluble unity, and sanctifies the spouses" (*The Church Teaches*—Documents of the Church in English Translation, sixth printing, St. Louis: B. Herder Book Co., 1964. No. 855, p. 336).

The emphasis on married love as the essence of Matrimony, however, is new in several respects:

1) Sin darkens conjugal love. The curse of sin above all affected marriage. Adam and Eve became mutually guilty of sin. They did not receive each other and their togetherness from God in a spirit of humble adoration. Consequently Adam's contempt: "It was the woman you put me with . . ." (Gen. 3:12). Sin is re-

flected in polygamy (Gen. 4:19-24), in man's thirst for power over woman, in the double standard which permitted a man the very licentiousness and infidelity he forbade in woman. A change was brought about through the Good News of redemption, particularly with respect to the relationship between the sexes. A man experiences the grace of redemption when he ceases to domineer over his wife and begins to love her with the unselfish love with which Christ loved His Church (Eph. 5:25). In a patriarchal social milieu, a woman lived the mystery of salvation to its fullest when she fulfilled her role with humility and love. But the more deeply redemption affects the entire life, the more woman's complete equality and dignity are recognized in the partnership of marriage. Redemption will be felt, again and again, as the completely new sound and accent of love.

2) The social and economic conditions of past centuries often clouded the meaning of conjugal love. The absolutism of princes was largely reflected in the position of the male as the head of the family. Family interests, and frequently mere economic considerations, determined the choice of marriage partners to such an extent that frequently the heads of families chose the marriage partner for their child and bargained about the "marriage contract." Although the marriage contract somehow included the core of Matrimony, its obvious purpose often was above all a business transaction between two families. Today, at least in the Western world, the choice of partners is the fundamental right of young people. The families may actively counsel, as

long as they do not endanger the young people's freedom of choice. Moreover, the choice of a partner no longer affects the economic and social interests of the two families as it did in past centuries. Thus, conjugal love comes to prominence.

3) In past centuries, life was normally restricted to the more intimate family, with several generations living together. Interpersonal relationships had a determining role due to the close interdependence of the economic and social structures. Modern man, on the other hand, spends a large part of his life in the anonymous realm of today's mass society and impersonal business world. In such a social atmosphere, man feels himself only partially fulfilled as a person. Personal friendship and, above all, the intimate realm of marriage and family assume new importance. Thus, modern personalism, particularly in a form emphasizing the I-you-we relationship, is an expression of the new approach to life—which, to be sure, allows for a variety of realizations running from a superficial sentimentalism to the most mature forms of cheerful and self-sacrificing mutual dedication.

4) Formerly, couples desired the highest possible number of children, even though they might not have loved each other too much. A great number of children meant economic and social status and the only possible form of old-age insurance. Of course, a good education, even in those days, was possible only when both parents truly loved each other. Today, economic and social considerations tempt the egoist to drastically limit the size of his family. It is getting

more and more obvious that, under the new conditions of life, only the most devoted conjugal love is an effective motive to have as many children as one can properly raise and educate.

5) In view of today's knowledge of the Bible, of modern psychology and anthropology, the previously held opinion that the marital act has fundamentally no purpose other than begetting children is untenable and scandalous. It is acknowledged more and more that the full expression of the conjugal union is one of the foundations of the human "word"—an expression of an irrevocable oneness. It has reference, therefore, to fruitfulness in the fullest human sense. Presenting, as alternatives, either having a child or indulging in mere selfish lust has always been a deplorable misunderstanding of the marital act. Today, it is getting increasingly clearer that such an attitude is inhuman and unchristian. Many times, prolonged and forcefully kept total abstinence, together with negligence of marital tenderness, not only provokes grave temptations against marital fidelity (cf. I Cor. 7:5), but often enough causes tensions and aggressiveness in one or both partners; via subconscious channels, it often turns into something like "psychological sterilization." One need only think of a young mother who concentrates all her affection on her baby while, misunderstanding marital chastity, she refuses signs of affection to her husband. The husband, then, will unconsciously develop a tendency to avoid such a rival for the affection and attentions of his wife.

Children Are No Incidental Matter

The marital calling is, essentially, a calling to parenthood; but surely, this does not imply that a marriage is meaningless or even cursed when it is not blessed with children. Emphatically the Council said: "Marriage, to be sure, is not instituted solely for procreation. . . . Therefore, marriage persists as a whole manner and communion of life, and maintains its value and indissolubility, even when offspring are lacking— despite, rather often, the very intense desire of the couple" (*Pastoral Constitution on the Church in the Modern World*, Art. 50). Conjugal love is in itself a praise of God's love and a high value in itself; but it is also necessary with respect to the parents' love for their children. As partners in the care and love for their children and in reciprocating their children's love, the husband and wife will grow in mutual affection and esteem. Their physical oneness, likewise—even when it is not actually for the purpose of awakening new life—receives a special fullness and dignity in view of their parental calling.

The True Face of Love

In a fundamentally Christian perspective, it is not correct to say that other virtues besides love are necessary in marriage. Everything else, if it is genuinely felt, does not stand in addition to married love, but is rather an expression of genuine love.

Genuine love between the spouses is strong, sincere and tender. It is respectful and considerate, benevolent and grateful; joyous, unselfish and ready to make sacrifices; for that very reason it is itself a fountain of joy; it is gentle and grateful for forbearance, faithful and anxious to make fidelity easy for the partner. It cannot be embittered. It rejoices in the truth which they recognize together and make more accessible to each other. "Love . . . is always ready to excuse, to trust, to hope, and to endure whatever comes" (I Cor. 13:7). Married love is the source of fruitfulness. It experiences its blessing in the harmonious education of children who, to that love, owe not only their lives, but also their capacity to love and to do good.

Christian love proves its worth in forgiveness. One of the greatest injustices one spouse can commit against the other is infidelity; but the innocent partner will make a humble examination of his own conscience to see whether he or she is not coresponsible for the guilt of the other; it may be due to a lack of tender consideration, a refusal of affection.

Great love will always prevail. It knows how to pray and live according to the words of the Our Father: "Forgive us our trespasses as we forgive those who trespass against us." God's faithfulness manifests itself in forgiveness. Forgiving love—which itself asks humbly for forgiveness, even where the evidence indicates that one's own guilt is of a lesser degree—celebrates the greatest triumphs on earth and wins the final victory for all eternity.

The love of the redeemed is redeeming love—a love which is salvific in imitation and collaboration with the Redeemer's love for all His brothers and sisters. Sanctified by the sacrament, conjugal love and love for one's children receive a special calling to reciprocal helpfulness along the road to salvation.

Yet, concern for salvation must be neither an adjunct to conjugal love nor a bare, optional superstructure, much less a substitute for loving kindness, understanding and tenderness. The "pious" wife who keeps her husband emotionally starved, who neglects both home and kitchen, adds to the disaster if she lectures to him on religion and virtue. However, a few words about God from a loving wife will bear fruit.

The grace of the sacrament of Matrimony becomes a great blessing for the children, if their parents have truly learned to love each other increasingly through all the vicissitudes of life, and if, together, they have manifested the true face of love to their children.

Questions for Further Discussion

1. Draw out the implications in the author's statement that it is in the family where religion and life are either integrated or condemned to hopeless separation.

2. What is the true meaning of the expression *"ex opere operato"* as used in the sacraments? How has the meaning sometimes been distorted in practice?

3. Contrast the emphasis of the Council and contemporary theology on the sacredness of conjugal love with the negative treatment sometimes given in the past.

4. What is the full meaning of the statement that the marital calling is a calling to parenthood?

5. Describe the many facets of true married love.

VIII
Responsible Parenthood

Our grandparents or at least our great-grandparents expressed their faith and their confidence in Divine Providence with the expression: "Children are accepted as God sends them," or "What God sends is well provided for." There was nothing wrong with this attitude.

In those days, the pace of life was much slower and people were not as worried about life in general as we are today. There was a time when man cultivated neither a garden nor a field. Then followed many thousands of years of simple hoe cultivation, and then, many years of primitive agriculture. Our modern scientific agriculture is something completely new and different in comparison to the preceding eras. Already, nations must plan ahead together, seeking ways to feed the world's population. Return to the level of the primitive fruit gatherer, or even to unscientific agriculture, would mean nothing less than mass suicide of humanity. However, this is not to say that there may not still be families in a few remote areas of Africa or even of the Abruzzi who try to survive with the methods of prescientific agriculture.

It is not arbitrariness, then, but rather the result of the radical changes in the life of man, in his biological condition, his psychological reactions, his tasks and his knowledge that prompt spouses to ask themselves in all honesty whether they may have another child. If, two or three generations ago, one desired about five adult children, then in view of the high infant mortality rate in those days, one had to aim at about 15 births. Most children did not need any vocational training; very early in life they made themselves useful around a farm or the workshop of an artisan. Rarely did a doctor dare to predict that a new pregnancy would imperil the life of the mother. One simply did not ask this question. It just did not seem to belong to the realm of human responsibility. Today, parents who would expect about 15 births, providing they have a relatively early marriage and normal fertility, have to take stock of themselves, asking whether or not they will be in a position to provide these children with an adequate education.

In contemporary USA, about one-third of the younger generation receives a college education. The fact that the American Negro has not yet had the same chances to benefit from the educational boom poses one of the most serious social problems. Similarly, the fact that only about three percent of the population in Latin America receives a college education forestalls the quick socioeconomic development so necessary to meet the rapidly increasing population.

"Where Does That Leave Belief In Divine Providence?"

During a committee meeting where responsible parenthood was the main topic, a pious old archbishop jumped up like an Old Testament prophet and shouted: "Where does that leave your belief in Divine Providence? Have you not read: '. . . I am telling you not to worry about your life and what you are to eat, nor about your body and how you are to clothe it. Surely, life means more than food, and the body more than clothing! Look at the birds in the sky. They do not sow or reap or gather into barns; yet your heavenly Father feeds them. Are you not worth much more than they are?' " (Matt. 6:25-26). What about the normative value of the Sermon on the Mount?

If Christ and the Apostles were living today, they would certainly preach the same religious truths, but not with the same words and parables nor with the same culture in mind. It will always be true that the disciple of Christ is not to give in to chronic worry. But he can no longer afford to dream of a Sabbath year during which there will be neither sowing nor reaping. Today we are no less in the hands of Divine Providence than those people at the time of the Sermon on the Mount. However, Divine Providence has entrusted us with different insights and means. If we do our share and make responsible use of the means by planning and foresight, then we can leave the rest up to the hand of Providence. Whatever may come, it will turn into something good for those who love God. But if we simply twiddle our thumbs, then we are sinning against Divine Providence.

When I nursed patients suffering from typhoid fever during the spring and summer of 1944 in the Pripet Marshes of Russia, when I vaccinated the people and separated the wells for the healthy from those of the sick, I heard the Orthodox say: "This priest loves us; but who knows whether he has the right faith; he does not seem to believe that sickness is sent by God and does not come out of wells or toilets!" These pious old farmers from the Pripet Marshes and that pious archbishop from Sicily express their faith in a language, imagination and limitation of human responsibility which is anything but fitting in this scientific era. They believe in God, but only in a God who ruled the prescientific world, not in the God of history who leads mankind through different stages and who demands man's full cooperation in accordance with a specific stage of knowledge and needs.

As long as a husband was unable to have any idea about the dangers involved in a new pregnancy for his wife, he was justified in not feeling guilty when his wife died or became mentally ill. However, if today he is told by a competent gynecologist, "Your wife needs at least two years of rest unless you want to endanger her health," then a serious question of conscience arises on the basis of this information. If he ignores these warnings, and if, then, his wife winds up in a mental institution with a serious case of postpartum psychosis, he cannot project the blame on Divine Providence. It was this very Providence which enabled him to understand the seriousness of the situation.

The Second Vatican Council points out to modern man how he must adjust himself to Divine Providence in marriage: "Parents should regard as their proper mission the task of transmitting human life and educating those to whom it has been transmitted. They should realize that they are thereby cooperators with the love of God the Creator, and are, so to speak, the interpreters of that love" (*Pastoral Constitution on the Church in the Modern World,* Art. 50). Any arbitrariness must be excluded from the deliberations of responsible parenthood. Yet this is not to say that parents, who are solely competent to decide on the desirable number of children, should not allow a certain leeway for freedom of judgment, for more or less courageous ventures.

The Christian and the New Consciousness

Modern city planning and modern scientific agriculture are challenges to both the believer and the unbeliever. One does not have to remain on the level of primitive fruit gathering or of simple hoe cultivation in order to be faithful. To be sure, the Christian will have additional thoughts about city planning when he realizes how much the development of personality and morality depends on cultured living.

Similarly, the modern consciousness in respect to the transmission of human life is, on a certain level of development, common to both believer and unbeliever. Both decide on the proper time, on the desirable intervals between individual pregnancies. It becomes a matter of conscious decision. The superficial, practical-minded unbeliever will degrade this decision to a mere calculation: "Should we have another child this year or should we buy a color TV set or a new car?" Truly faithful and mature married couples, however, respond to a divine calling in their considered decision to transmit new life and to raise a child properly. They consider themselves cooperators with the love of the Creator. Their decision assumes the character of a loving response to God, a loving answer to the desires and genuine possibilities of the spouses and the entire family. They will not once and for all set the limits early in their married life: two children —that is it. They will keep themselves forever open for the gifts of divine love. If their conjugal love, their harmony, their skill in rearing children, and their delight in each other and in their children grow, then their spontaneous gratitude to God will frequently be expressed in their desire for another child.

Modern equalitarianism likes to predetermine how many children one ought to have: "Two, three at the most." Birth control at any price, with the idea of keeping all families small, frequently originates among the privileged classes; they are afraid that their high living standard might somehow be imperiled by the fertility of the masses. They are opposed to foreign aid and preach, therefore—at a considerable cost—drastic methods of birth planning to the rapidly developing nations of Asia and Africa.

The responsible parenthood of faithful and mature Christians shares with the advocates of birth control and equalitarian birth planning only the awareness of and the attitude toward these questions. The mental set and its moral result, however, are as different as night and day. In no way is a Christian always under the obligation to have many children. A mother of one child who has suffered several miscarriages really has risked much and has done the maximum. Others, even after the eighth or ninth child, might still desire another one without determining that this should be the last one. The Second Vatican Council clearly favors consciously responsible parenthood and praises the family with many children; however, this is encouraged provided that it be the result of a "wise and common deliberation." The parents must also be in a position to bring up suitably even a relatively large family (*Pastoral Constitution on the Church in the Modern World,* Art. 50). Well-raised and well-educated children surely will not aggravate the population problem.

The moment that can transmit new life is transformed into a moment of generous decision for responsible parents when they accept the ensuing sacrifices and restrictive measures; at the same time, it will also be the source of many joys for a good many years. The transmission of human life possesses no intrinsic moral value unless it expresses the acceptance of the totality of the parental calling. It devolves upon the parents to bring up their children to be responsible and mature citizens of the world and the Church. In a pluralistic and highly differentiated dynamic society where practically everything undergoes constant change, rearing children requires much greater skill than was called for with the static and closed social conditions of the past. Thus the concept of "responsible parenthood" includes the added duty of preparing oneself thoroughly, the duty of acquiring—both before and during the years of marriage—the needed pedagogical knowledge. The Christian Family Movement and similar family groups figure prominently in this respect, for there, ideally minded families share on a small scale their counsel, encouragement and help.

Birth Control—But How?

Consciously responsible procreation poses the question of how to control births. This issue is disputed no less hotly, but certainly no more, than other issues in the course of history: no more than the question of the justification of torture when it was still practiced by the Inquisition, the question related to the burning of "witches" after a papal bull insisted upon it, the question of direct power of the Church in the temporal (political) realm, of the question of usury after the modern economic reform reevaluated the lending of money in accordance with its new meaning and function. Both moral theologians and believers will probably be confronted with new problematic questions again and again until the second advent of Christ. It is true because of human history, which *e pur si muove* ("and yet it moves"—Galileo), and because there will always be those among us who would rather see the world not move at all. Galileo and his opponents will not have to complain about a lack of successors.

The current discussions going on in the Church are rather confusing to many. That is why some people would have theologians remain silent. Undoubtedly, this would be the most convenient solution; indeed! Yet, is this responsible in view of the din of mass communications media: radio, newspapers, films and everyday discussions? It is the principal task of the theologian to study these questions thoroughly, to discuss them with experts, to listen to laymen, especially those known for their particular competency in certain fields of the sciences. Yet, since this issue is debated at every street corner, on every wave length, and since some Christians might arrive at the most dangerous conclusion that everything has become doubtful, it is the duty of the theologian to state the argument clearly, delineating— in the essential aspects—what is not up for discussion, at least insofar as Catholic theology is concerned.

The sacred right to life of every human being is beyond any debate. "Therefore from the moment of its conception, life must be guarded with the greatest care, while abortion and infanticide are unspeakable crimes" (*Pastoral Constitution on the Church in the Modern World,* Art. 51). The dilemma of the moral theologian consists only in the fact that there do, indeed, exist certain borderline cases in which everything must be done to save the lives of both mother and child. An operation is not to be called an abortion in the strict moral sense (i.e., does not deprive the child of its right to life) if a competent obstetrician, in his function as the interpreter of Divine Providence, seeing that the child has no chance to survive, determines to save the life of the mother. These extreme cases have become fewer and fewer in recent years.

There is general agreement concerning the problem of sterilization, at least insofar as the essential aspects are concerned. Any arbitrary destruction or mutilation of human fertility must definitely be denied. Scientific doubts concern only those cases where the health of the entire person calls for an operation. This was generally called, then, "indirect sterilization." There are extreme cases where expert interpretation of the situation clearly arrives at the conclusion that, on the level of natural law—that is to say, a rational evaluation of the facts and of human responsibility — any further fertility must be eliminated for good. An operation performed with these realizations in mind (in order to save a life or a marriage) would, then, in a moral sense, not be a sterilization properly so called, since it is not a destruction of responsible human fertility; responsible reasoning would exclude it anyhow. Yet these are extreme cases.

One possible solution to the problem of birth control is total abstinence. However, this calls for a tremendous amount of self-control in every respect and it can be beneficial to a marriage only if it works hand in hand with a conscious and careful observance of tender married love.

It is highly important to understand clearly that total abstinence is not a value in itself, especially if its motive is selfishness or coldness. All the methods of birth control are of no avail unless they are accompanied by a genuine spirit of responsibility.

At Corinth, St. Paul had to deal with married people who, in an enthusiasm typical of converts, decided on total abstinence, partly however, because of their expectation of a near second coming of the Lord. The Apostle warns them: "Do not refuse each other except for mutual consent, and then only for an agreed time, to leave yourselves free for prayer; then come together again lest

Satan tempt you through lack of self-control" (I Cor. 7:5).

The Council fully realized that it is not so simple to offer total abstinence as *the* solution to all married people. "But where the intimacy of married life is broken off, it is not rare for its faithfulness to be imperiled and its quality of fruitfulness ruined. For then the upbringing of the children and the courage to accept new ones are both endangered" (*Constitution on the Church in the Modern World*, Art. 51).

The least one can surmise from this text is that married people should never refuse each other the expression of marital tenderness, particularly when the circumstances call for a prolonged period of abstinence. Any fear of sexual excitement as a consequence of mutual tenderness must be overcome. Yet, it is absolutely necessary to understand that genuine marital tenderness, as intimate as it might be, has nothing in common with the widespread necking and petting practices of unmarried people. Such petting is rather a mutual sexual exploitation, even though there might be an agreement to go only so far. Marital tenderness is something very special and it is totally different from premarital sex: It is the genuine and respectful expression of togetherness, of mutual loving attention, and vigilance.

As early as 1951, Pope Pius XII already approved of periodic abstinence (the rhythm method) as a means of birth regulation, although noted theologians — for example, F. Hürth — thought that it was immoral to consciously choose the infertile days as a means of birth control (Address to the Midwives of Italy). However,

Pius XII was very specific about the fact that the motives ought to be the decisive factor. Married people act correctly only if they have sound reasons not to desire any more children at a given time.

Since 1951, periodic abstinence as a method of birth regulation has developed into a highly complicated technique with calendar, body temperature control, observance of abdominal pain, chemical analysis of the vaginal flow and medical counseling. This method was praised from many pulpits as the "Catholic method" and considered as highly safe. Because a certain cardinal spoke more frequently about these issues than about the Paschal mystery and because he hailed this method as being "safe" and dependable, he was popularly called the "cardinal-safe-period."

One must not overlook that it was Pius XII who initiated discussions with new aspects of these issues within the Church. His decision left no doubts about the fact that marital intercourse is good and remains so as an expression and furtherance of married love, harmony and faithfulness, even though the spouses try to sever the intercourse effectively from any possible unwanted pregnancy by means of a calculating method, provided that they have sufficient reasons for doing so. Moreover, the (partly erroneous) praises given to the safety of this method by many bishops, theologians, priests and laymen, made it perfectly clear that a method of birth control is not bad *per se,* just because it is effective.

Yet, it was impossible to avoid the issue: "Why is this method morally good and why are those formerly condemned methods morally bad?"

Some gave the following answer: "Because this method does not interfere with the physiological processes of the marital act and its consequences."

The argument frequently raised against this position was: "This method is an interference, after all, indeed a rather radical interference, into the psychological processes which are of higher quality and even more important to man in his entirety than mere physiological processes. Moreover, the objective is the same with reference to the physiological processes, that is, to prevent the union of sperm and egg during an actual marital act."

Another answer was: "This method is better than earlier condemned methods, because it does not tamper with the expressiveness and dignity of the marital act." This answer is certainly more convincing than the other that focuses only on the "inviolability of biological processes," but it gives rise to new questions: "What if some recently developed methods do preserve the dignity and integrity of the marital act and are certainly far from having to do with abortion?"

At this point in the discussion, the Council text on marriage and family was worked out. Most important of all, one must see how the question is stated now: that of harmonizing the needs of conjugal love with the responsible transmission of life.

The first statement of the Council is that the good end does not simply justify the means—an old Catholic principle which is rather topical in comparison with a chaotic ethics which tries to approve everything, including abortion (e.g., Joseph Fletcher, *Situation Ethics*). In addition, the Council offers positive criteria: "Therefore, when there is question of harmonizing conjugal love with the responsible transmission of life, the moral aspect of any procedure does not depend solely on sincere intentions or on an evaluation of motives. It must be determined by objective standards. These, based on the nature of the human person and his acts, preserve the full sense of mutual self-giving and human procreation in the context of true love" *Constitution on the Church in the Modern World,* Art. 51). Upon the wish of Pope Paul, it was pointed out: "Such a goal cannot be achieved unless the virtue of conjugal chastity is sincerely practiced." This is of great importance. It must be clearly understood that the development of the doctrines of the Church and the answers to new questions cannot be a matter of watering down Christian morality. The criteria listed by the Council demand of every spouse a constant vigilance with regard to the true nature of the marital act, mutual respect, and frequently, the mortification of selfish tendencies.

Yet it cannot be overlooked that the Council did not even touch on that criterion which seemed to be the only decisive one according to a traditionalist concept, that is, the absolute inviolability of physiological processes which would have to characterize every single marital act as a potential act of procreation. Certainly, the Council Fathers would not have omitted to emphasize this criterion if it had been an unquestionable criterion in their eyes (in their entirety or majority).

The famous footnote 14, which makes reference to the rather strict formulations of *Casti Connubii*, cannot simply be interpreted as an affirmation and reemphasis of these formulations given forty years ago, since the same footnote also mentions the comparatively revolutionary address of Pope Pius XII and an address delivered by Pope Paul VI on June 23, 1964, which announced the existence of a papal commission for the study of the issues involved, yet warned against too hasty hopes for a change in the directives of the Church. It goes without saying that neither laymen nor theologians will have the final say in these matters: It will be up to the pope alone. Popes have had the final say about the permissibility of moderate usury, about the nonexistence of a direct power of the Church in temporal and political matters, about the immorality of witch hunts and torture. Thereby they corrected fallible announcements of preceding popes who, because of a different historical context, did neither see nor discern clearly. But the entire people of God somehow were instrumental in the final clarification through prayer, study or experience. Individual theologians decisively initiated the useful and necessary distinctions. At the end of a period of development, it was always clear that the moral values stated in previous documents of the Church were not only preserved, but even better clarified through finer distinctions and sometimes corrections.

The decisive values relative to marital chastity, which were mainly protected by the past tradition of the Church and which must always be protected, appear to me to be the following:

(1) It is a blessing for a man to be born; procreation is basically good.

(2) The transmission of life and upbringing in the family must be envisioned in their entirety and interdependence. It is not good to procreate unless there is the will and the possibility to educate the child properly.

(3) The marital act and its dignity are of high moral significance.

(4) The life of a child is inviolable beginning with the moment of conception.

Under the still controversial assumption that not every interference with the physiological realm is immoral, the following tentative guidelines for a solution might be considered: If an act of birth regulation is in the interest of the person (of the spouses as persons and of their genuine interpersonal relationship) and if it is necessary, then that action must be preferred which, all things considered, is the most dignified and which preserves the total meaning of the marital act best. Points for consideration include marital faithfulness, the continuation of the marriage, the atmosphere of harmony and love which is so necessary for the education of children, the readiness of desire for further children at the proper time. Thereby, the differences in personality and cultural background must be given due consideration. Moral solutions which can only be offered to privileged strata and nations are suspect in view of the Gospel. A moral theologian must always have the underprivileged and the poor in mind, for the salvation, the gradual progress and dignity of *every* human being, is at stake!

What I said represents merely an attempt which, to be sure, is gaining wider and wider recognition. Many questions are yet left open. The entire people of God, above all those who possess special knowledge, experience and intuition, must continue to investigate how, under given conditions, the full meaning of marital devotion and the readiness to joyfully fulfill the marital calling can be preserved and furthered. Once again, it must be clearly understood that the final word is up to the teaching authority in the Church whenever fundamental moral aspects are involved. Reverence for the majesty of truth that must be sought carefully and unflinchingly, and for the authority of the successor of Peter and the bishops of the world, bind us in duty to remain patient. Doctrinal solutions cannot be achieved overnight, nor is it possible to bury vital issues. Questions which are not yet ripe should be left open.

If we all clearly realize the abundance of lasting values and principles, if we develop and cultivate them in full vigilance and if we regard the controversies with Christian prudence, vigilance, humility and patience, then the present discussions cannot do us any harm; rather, they become a call to thoroughness, to a more mature and at the same time more demanding and understanding morality.

Questions for Further Discussion

1. Describe the radical changes in the life of man in terms of biology, psychology, socioeconomic development, and the gain in knowledge of these matters that have influenced him to limit the number of his offspring. Why does not such planning deny belief in Divine Providence?

2. How do the approaches of the true believer and the unbeliever differ in the matter of birth planning? What does it mean that the proper transmission of human life must express "the acceptance of the totality of the parental calling"?

3. Why is it necessary to see the controverted question on birth control in the proper historical context? Is the question more difficult than some previous issues in the Church?

4. Outline what the author states as the argument on the issue of birth control, giving also what is not up for discussion. What are the solutions he proposes?

5. How, in the Council's terms, are the needs of conjugal love harmonized with the responsible transmission of life?

6. Discuss the "tentative guidelines" for a solution the author gives.

IX
Family Relationships

Although God's commandment: "Honor your father and your mother" (Ex. 20-12) is addressed to men of all times and places, the fulfillment of this charge is greatly conditioned by man's historical setting. It is the task of both speculative and applied ethics to present principles of moral conduct within the general framework of lasting values. Today we are fully aware of the far-reaching influence which the "father image" exerts on both the conscious and unconscious levels of man's religious conscience. The full realization of this truth urges us to rid ourselves of an obsolete and distorted father image in both morality and religion.

It would be beyond the competence of empirical psychology to infer from Freud's psychoanalytical experiences that the son invariably develops a kind of Oedipus complex and that a secret rebellion against his father gives impetus to his psychological energies. On the other hand, it cannot be denied that very early in life dangerous conflicts, not only against one's earthly father but against all authority figures including that of the heavenly Father, may develop in the deepest recesses of the child's psychological experiences.

In a similar manner, early childhood experiences with a tyrannical and overly strict father are the roots of irrational disproportionate guilt complexes. Deep-seated rebellion against a feudalistic or paternalistic "father image" of the Church often goes hand in hand with an overt rebellion against any despotic or outdated exercise of parental authority. One of the principal sources for social tensions, for distorted personalities, and for unbelief and rebellion against the Church, arises from the stubborn adherence to old-fashioned regimes in the exercise of authority in the family, in the Church, and in society at large. The paternalistic "ruler" or "prince of the Church" patterned after the despotic age of his forefathers, who in all matters poses as the infallible representative of God, becomes an insurmountable obstacle to man's search for God.

Family Life — a Partnership

In primitive society, woman played a significant role in providing sustenance to the family through the tilling of the soil in gardens and fields. A husband left father and mother to follow his wife and her maternal clan. However, with the introduction of domesticated animals and improved methods of agriculture, man emerged as the undisputed manager of a predominantly paternal family. The book of Genesis considers the dominion of man over woman the result of original sin and, at the same time, symbolic of man's need for redemption (cf. Gen. 3:17). We see this wrong attitude in the worst form when Lamech, the descendant of Cain, married two women and tyrannized them (cf. Gen. 4:19-24). Man, after gaining superiority over woman, also invented the double standard in morality. This is seen in the ancient law where the unfaithful woman was condemned to die, while the equally guilty man was left to go unpunished.

The position of woman was favorably influenced by the religious ideas expressed in God's covenant with His chosen people — a covenant which takes its imagery from the love relationship between husband and wife. In the light of the sacramental dignity of marriage, the redeemed husband is called to a humble love similar to that of Our Lord for His Church. Thereby man becomes liberated and redeemed from his selfish desire to rule over his wife. Thus religion attacked the faulty and debasing structures of ancient family life even before the time of full social reform. The Gospel teaches a new attitude to women, although the New Testament is still abounding in many admonitions regarding obedience and subjection for women. This was in keeping with the prevailing conditions of family life and social institutions of that time. In our modern civilization, family life has become a system of partnership. Husband and wife mutually listen and express their opinions so that decisions by consent can be achieved. They mutually relinquish selfish desires where a compromise is needed. Mere autocratic ruling, on the part of the husband as the lord of the house, undermines his true moral authority.

The times are gone when a girl is given in marriage by her father. Today the choice of marriage partners is a mutual one between two young people. Their relationship is characterized by reciprocal respect and devotion so essential to a community of perfect partnership.

In our desire for an ultimate resolution of

social and religious tensions in today's society, we should concentrate our efforts toward a fuller implementation of the partnership idea to all realms of life. There is no doubt that priests and bishops, raised in families where inter-personal relationships were characterized by the idea of partnership, will have a different ap-proach to the exercise of their authority when compared with members of the clergy coming from autocratic and paternalistic families where the wife and children were kept in the role of servants and where the son impatiently waited for the day of emancipation when he could rule his own family.

The whole pattern of today's democratic style of living largely determines the mutual relation-ships between parents and children. Children should be helped to mature gradually to share in family partnership and social responsibility. In past ages where young people even after their marriage remained within the patriarchal struc-ture, the raising of children primarily aimed at obedience and loyalty to the clan. Today such practices would have serious consequences for both the individual and society. Today our aim must be the education of children toward an ever-maturer sharing of responsibility.

Authority and Obedience

Past approaches to obedience in both teach-ing and practice were extremely one-sided. They failed to stress the truly Christian meaning of authority and its genuine exercise. Guides for the examination of conscience abounded in cate-gories of sins for those ruled, while no matter for the examination of conscience was included for rulers such as Church dignitaries (popes and bishops), religious superiors, or worldly dignitaries and executives. How could a person rendering such passive and unenlightened obedience ever be expected to mature into the role of the superior and effectively discharge his duties?

God's authority is primarily one of love, based on the inscrutable decrees of divine wisdom to call creatures into being in order to make them the concelebrants of His own divine love. Freedom in our relationship to God connotes a grateful acceptance of His dominion and authority. It is important to note that God does not demand an obedience of slaves. He made us His free sons and daughters. God preferred to create man free even at the risk of a possible misuse of that freedom, rather than to subject him to blind and slavish obedience. Through his own selfish disobedience, man jeopardized the integrity of his God-given freedom. On the other hand, Christ's redemption calls man to a freedom of loving obedience. By a mutual and all-embracing love, we participate in God's freedom as His sons and daughters. As children of God, we are given the basic guidelines for this freedom. Christ solemnly announced: "This is my commandment: love one another, as I have loved you. . . . I shall not call you servants any more, because a servant does not know his master's business; I call you friends, because I have made known to you everything I have learnt from my Father" (John 15:12-15).

God the Father is the eternal source of Christ's magnitude of love and filial freedom. The Son's own love for us is designed to lead

124

us to the Father, the source of all authority. His love is life-giving and authoritative. Christ's commandment of love extends beyond the mere "Thou shalt"; it embraces the motivation, the power and the authority of love: "As the Father has loved me, so I have loved you. Remain in my love" (John 15:9). Ultimately, the commandment of love receives its meaning and its liberating and binding force only in view of Christ's love. His love invites us to reciprocate His charity in an all-embracing exercise of love. The very authority of Christ is rooted in His love. The fulfillment of Christ's new commandment becomes easy if we unite ourselves with His charity. Thus obedience becomes personal fulfillment in an increasing freedom.

Parental authority, in analogy to the Creator's and Redeemer's love, must be a life-giving love. It has its roots in the conjugal love which makes parents accept and desire children so that they might become the concelebrants of their own love. If parents fail to accept the child as a person in a genuine and wholehearted love, their authority becomes void of true authenticity. Their God-ordained authority becomes even more marred if they arbitrarily enforce their authority in order to "break their children's will" instead of guiding them to a free and responsible type of obedience which is based on understanding and insight.

Today, more than ever before, parental authority should provide an atmosphere conducive to individual initiative and freedom. Therefore, parents should refrain from literally smothering their children with commands and restrictions in so many do's and don'ts. They should not surround the adolescent with excessive regulations. In other words, they ought to help their children toward greater independence even at the risk of errors and mistakes. We certainly should not provide a favorable environment for errors and blunders. Yet all of us, whether we want it or not, will make a certain number of mistakes. Similar to learning a new language, we are unable to learn it unless we take the risk of learning it through trials and errors. On the other hand, the courage to make mistakes without the initiative to learn from our experience is likewise doomed to failure. Young people need encouragement and a fair amount of freedom of action with a fair amount of supervision.

Today some of the Church's critics are rather arrogant. Proposals for reform and critical judgments are presented in a tone of certain infallibility. This syndrome, on the whole, can be compared with the stage of development in puberty when the human being, on awakening to a fuller self-consciousness, will act with an air of increasing infallibility as he perceives the established order of society and the bearers of authority impose their commands and opinions as infallible laws. An autocratic manner of imposing authority in the family and the Church tends to undermine the very roots of the established order. This is probably due to both a subconscious and unconscious process in man. If, on the other hand, parents would present their opinions with modesty and simplicity, admitting their own mistakes, there would be less arrogance in adolescents. Just as filial arrogance is found with "infallible" parents, so likewise in the

Church we find the most severe criticism and tensions in the dioceses and provinces of "infallible" bishops and superiors. Modesty in the exercise of authority is more likely to produce sincere obedience than the constant pounding on one's authority.

Those who expect the pope to make clear declarations of infallibility or clear-cut statements in matters pertaining to natural law, that is to say in issues involving divine revelation, have failed to recognize the true functions of authority as taught by social psychology. Similarly misled are those who fail to take the pronouncements of the pope or the Council seriously, unless these are spoken in terms of infallibility. A rather authoritarian type of archbishop, quite vocal in his criticism of Pope John and the Ecumenical Council, when questioned as to his allegiance and obedience to the Church, responded that the Council has not spoken with infallibility and consequently cannot oblige him to allegiance and obedience. It is hoped that the so-called "liberals" in the Church will not subscribe to such a kind of "selective disobedience" which is found in the authoritarian reactionaries. Humble obedience is possible only where a truly humble exercise of authority is found. Such humble obedience will never be blind but rather enlightened in regard to the innate limitations of one's own judgments. This requires an enlightened acceptance of unavoidable limitations in the one commanding, as well as a permissive attitude of those in authority, such as parents and Church leaders, so that children and the faithful at large can exercise a certain amount of spontaneity. Similarly, children have to be permissive with their parents and their limitations. A sense of humor is a wonderful asset to the Christian, especially if the bishops, or even the pope, should act or speak in ways less perfect than expected.

The Dialogue Between the Generations

Any crisis of authority and obedience is usually associated with the problems between the older and younger generations. This problem is more exaggerated today because various age groups subscribe to different outlooks on life. Young people speak an entirely different language although they may have some concepts in common with the older generation. The style of life for the younger generation greatly differs from that of the middle-aged and senior citizens. Youth is critical of both institutions and customs when such appear phony, formalistic and empty. The younger generation's protest against obsolete laws and regulations should not be considered as rebellion against authority or the established order and morality.

In reality, the qualities of the different generations should be complimentary and therefore a potential positive factor. The resulting tension between the different age groups may stimulate progress in continuity, and likewise continuity in progress. Tensions may become truly fruitful, in a Christian sense, if they are approached and resolved in the spirit of love, patience and mutual respect.

The fundamental law for the dialogue between the generations is that of mutual listening so that issues, which unite as well as separate us, can be properly evaluated. We may find a common background, a common concern, or a common heritage, even in regard to points of disagreement. In addition to a sincere dialogue, we need a humble realization of a constantly expanding knowledge which can rectify and modify our own opinions.

In past ages, adolescents were expected to mature peacefully while adapting themselves to the traditional forms and customs of life. In the event of difficulties, it was invariably presumed that the organization or institution embodied the greater wisdom. It was an accepted truth that only youth needed to learn something. Granted that in this dynamic society the wisdom of the experienced and at the same time open-minded mature person is able to make a significant contribution, we should also recognize the special qualities which characterize the young, such as enthusiasm, initiative and a keen desire for a radical and genuine sincerity.

Our age demands of both young and old a mentality which not only tolerates differences of opinions, but tries to weigh and appreciate their positive values. In certain areas of mutual concern, united and immediate action with a fair compromise would be the best course of action. Even if young people are unable to share the appreciation for certain pious exercises or moral convictions of the older generation, they still should accept and respect these as meaningful expressions of their elders. Reciprocally, it would be well for adults to tolerate and respect the attitudes of the rising generation. I would like to illustrate the above by a personal experience: Last year when celebrating Holy Mass in the cathedral at Cuernavaca, Mexico, my German mentality was first displeased with the type of liturgical music and singing since it was genuinely Mexican and ultramodern. However, I immediately noticed that all this was very meaningful to the people and it seemed close to their real life. Therefore, I soon was completely taken over by their passionate display of faith which all of a sudden had become meaningful and significant even to me, a stranger.

Mutual Responsibility for Salvation

Christ endowed His Church with a definite pastoral character. This presupposes respective attitudes and a decidedly pastoral approach in all those charged with special responsibilities for the salvation of other members of the community. This, however, does not minimize or exclude the mutual pastoral concern and responsibility which is the duty of all Christians. At times, some members of the Christian community, endowed with special charisms and not burdened by offices and obligations, are in a better position to work for the salvation of their brethren than even the consecrated priest.

The same truth applies to pastoral concerns for one's family members. The spouses are basically responsible for each other's salvation as mutual shepherds of their souls. In addition, parents are the "first preachers of the faith to their children" (*Constitution on the Church*, Art. 11). It is their noble task to convey to their children the gladsome tidings of the Gospel and of the Christian life which was transmitted to them in Baptism. The parent's sincere respect for the personal dignity of each child, together with their sincere love and firm discipline, not only gives testimony of their own faith but confirms the faith in their children's hearts. Their example provides the child with firsthand experience of the nobility of a truly Christian life. Parents fulfill their priestly task when they make their family a community worshiping God in true faith, hope and confident love. We should never expect children to accept the message of the Gospel slavishly. Mutual acceptance in family living implies cooperation and collaboration in the "give and take" of daily life.

The *Pastoral Constitution on the Church in the Modern World* throws special light on the reciprocal character of man's responsibility in relation to authority. "Thus the family is a foundation of society. In it the various generations come together and help one another to grow wiser and to harmonize personal rights with the other requirements of social life" (*Pastoral Constitution on the Church in the Modern World,* Art. 52). It would be for the greatest benefit of our society if every member in the family were to recognize and accept his special role in behalf of the whole. Authority is at its best when it provides an atmosphere conducive to the full personality development through a reciprocal sharing of responsibility.

Parents are endowed with a special type of authority. Nevertheless, they reach their fulfillment only through a loving dependence on God's own authority. Docility and gratitude to

God tend to make parents open-minded and grateful to their own children. The Council states: "As living members of the family, children contribute in their own way to making their parents holy" (*Pastoral Constitution on the Church in the Modern World*, Art. 48). Children have a decided responsibility for the salvation of their parents which they can best meet within the realm of genuine love and gratitude.

Questions for Further Discussion

1. What does the author mean when he says that God's commandment to honor father and mother, while addressed to men of all times and places, "is greatly conditioned by man's historical setting"?

2. Discuss authority and obedience in today's understanding of family life as a partnership. Is it unrealistic to hold that children should have a say in family matters?

3. What values would you say young people have in common with the older generation? What values conflict?

4. How can the particular virtues of the young be best capitalized upon for the benefit of all of society and the world?

5. How do parents best educate their children toward an ever maturer sharing of responsibility?

X
Celibacy for the Sake of the Kingdom

In many civilizations, single life and childlessness have been considered a particularly harsh fate, if not a punishment from God. Christ spoke (cf. Matt. 19:12) of those who are incapable of marriage, "born so from their mother's womb" or "made so by man," whose continence means privation, suffering, and perhaps injustice. But distinct from them, He spoke also of the continence that is a free personal choice "for the sake of the kingdom of heaven." "Let him accept it who can," He said.

Accordingly, there has been in Christ's Church a continuing history of this voluntarily dedicated continence that is a gift of grace and a testimony to the blessedness of the kingdom of heaven. To appreciate the true nature of this continence, we must distinguish its essential and lasting message of salvation from conditions that result from the necessities and circumstances of an era.

Testimony to the Coming of the Kingdom of God

The synoptics describe Jesus' sermon as the message of the kingdom of God that comes with Him and through Him. God takes possession of the human heart. The manifestations of His love guide men and deliver them from an enslaving attachment to temporal things. The kingdom of God, the kingdom of heaven, is infinitely more than all the powers and forces of this world and this age. It extends beyond all earthly experience. Christ Himself does not derive His human nature and His mission here on earth from "flesh and blood," not from that most powerful of earthly forces, the union of man and woman. Neither does Christ, who is the final and perfect man, build His house and family on an earthly foundation. Those who have been chosen by Him to be the sons and daughters of God must recognize that they do not owe this privilege "to the urge of the flesh and the will of man" (cf. John 1:12). The kingdom of heaven is not merely the open future of a happy family and a better constituted society; it is the direct and immediate openness to life eternal.

The presence of the kingdom of heaven is perfectly shown in Christ Himself, in a life that goes beyond all that man has ever experienced or yearned for. Since the fullness of the Spirit rests with Him and He lives wholly for the Father, He does not think of Himself. He is not concerned to preserve His life. The splendor and power of earthly kingdoms are not for Him; nor does He choose the way of marriage, although He is more capable of love than any man ever was. His total commitment is to the will and the love of the Father and to an unconditional dedication to all men. The testimony of His celibacy must be seen in this totality through His sermons, in the testimony of His life, in the signs of the dominion of God and, above all, in the Easter mystery of death and resurrection.

There is no law imposed on the disciples of Christ to leave everything—father, mother, house, and wife—in order to follow Him in total dedication to the kingdom of heaven; it is their own free and joyous decision. Made today, this decision reflects the characteristics of the new era, of the new freedom and the new hope. The disciple who knows that he is only on pilgrimage here on this earth is already filled with the beatitudes. His heart yearns for only one thing: to please the Lord (cf. I Cor. 4:32), to concentrate all his energies on the propagation of the Good News and to dedicate himself to the service of brotherly love.

This enthusiastic self-liberation for the sake of the Lord and His Gospel is ultimately rooted, not in expectation of His *parousia* in a near future, but in the realization that the Lord and His dominion of love are already at hand. It is not the "shortness of time" that creates the urgency but the compressed and pressing fullness of this time of salvation in which the final coming of the Lord is prepared. The usual translation of I Cor. 7:29 as "the time is growing short" is open to criticism. Physical time would have to be rendered in Greek as *"chronos,"* whereas *"kairos"* is the hour of salvation, charged with divine energies. This is not only short for every man—for instance in comparison with eternal destiny—but "compressed," "fulfilled and pressing" (*synestalménos*). That is why this unique hour of salvation addresses both married and unmarried in the form of a gift and a call to radical freedom for the cause of the Lord.

Voluntary celibacy has special value as testimony to the urgency of the *kairos*. It is a charism, a blessed enthusiasm for the Good News of the dominion of God, a free and fervent dedication to His Gospel and the service thereof; it is total surrender to Christ and the coming of His kingdom.

In my opinion, it would be wrong to say simply that voluntary continence for the sake of the kingdom of heaven makes the person who chooses this life a better disciple of Christ than the one who marries. But since marriage precedes the coming of the kingdom of God as a natural choice of life, all those capable of marriage would ordinarily marry regardless of the impending dominion of God. Hence celibacy, freely chosen and joyfully experienced, is a particularly eloquent testimony to the blessedness of the Gospel and to the liberating and urgent impact of the coming of the kingdom.

The definition of the Council of Trent, according to which it must not be denied "that it is better and more blessed to remain single than to marry" (Session XXIV Canon 1, *Denzinger* No. 1910) must be interpreted, in my opinion, with the emphasis on "more blessed" (*beatius*). This "more blessed" cannot be grasped within the categories of a humanistic morality of self-perfection. Its meaning becomes wholly distorted in any context of earned spiritual status. Rather, this is God's own gift of a blessedness that pours out the Good News of the approaching kingdom of heaven; it is a special gift of the Holy Spirit: the blessedness of a charism in the service of the Gospel, or a witness for the kingdom.

Martyrdom and Celibacy

The celibacy of Christ must be seen in the light of His testimony (*martyrion*) in the Easter mystery. The announcement of the kingdom of God was most intimately connected with martyrdom during the days of the infant Church. The martyr witnessed in a unique way the power of faith as well as the Good News of the eternal kingdom whose reality could be already felt here and now. Since the days of the Apostles, a similar testimonial value has been attributed to consecrated celibacy, truly lived.

In the Constantinian era, when martyrdom had become a rarity and when many members of the official Church had established themselves in the earthly splendor of an imperial Church, and the descendants of the Apostles became princes of empire and "princes of the Church," the testimony of those who, in full freedom, chose poverty and a single life as their lot, assumed special value as a loving yet firm protest against the secularization of the Church. The testimony of monks and virgins withstood the tension between the eschatologically understood kingdom of God and the "princedom" of many a churchman and ecclesiastical institution, and did so without lapsing into rebellion against authority. The fact that popes and bishops, who themselves were enamored of the splendor, pageantry, power and privileges of a Church that leaned more and more toward worldliness, nevertheless approved of the testimony of the celibate, must not be underestimated from a religious point of view.

The celibacy of an ever-increasing number of monks in the East and in the West, of the bishops of the East and the entire clergy in the West, helped substantially in saving the Church from total corruption and the feudalism of powerful families. If at times, despite the still-existing celibacy of the priests, the Apostolic See and bishoprics became bones of contention and the sport of powerful families that fought over benefices, prebends and fiefs, how much worse the situation would have been if the ideal of celibacy had vanished entirely! The scandalous behavior of an Alexander VI who, though unmarried, could not care less about celibacy, and who appointed his son, the robber-chief Cesare Borgia, to be a cardinal, amply testifies to this danger.

To be sure, the Church benefited only to the extent that celibacy was really understood and embraced because of its intrinsic value. This will always be so, for it must ever be clearly seen that the law of celibacy, understood chiefly as a law or, even worse, misunderstood as a necessity for the freedom of the Church in a purely sociological sense, becomes valueless and absurd. Only its essential motivation measures the dimension of its testimony to the kingdom of heaven.

Social Recognition of Those Who Are Single

In the epoch of the family-group, when two or three generations lived under the same roof, an unmarried person had his place in this group and thus enjoyed social recognition and incorporation. The number of single people was relatively high during some periods in the past because the scope and number of family enterprises could not be increased at will in an agricultural society that had, to a considerable degree, already reached its saturation point. Those members of a family who remained single were usually welcomed and appreciated on the parental farm or in the parental workshop.

This social structure largely favored the spread of religious community life. One need only remember Ireland. During the past generations, a a large part of the population saw clearly that, unless they emigrated, they could never have families of their own. When the parental farm was small, it was simply not advisable to remain within one's own family. To choose the priesthood or life in a convent meant, in any case, social incorporation into a community whose model remained the family-group. Frequently it meant definite social advancement as well.

Beginning with the dawn of industrialization, the picture has changed fundamentally. As far as the economics of the situation is concerned, everyone who has learned a trade, indeed everyone who is healthy and willing to work, can now marry and have a family of his own. In our modern society, the right to marry is considered one of the most fundamental of human rights. But single people and those who do not belong to a religious family are not at all in the same position as their brothers and sisters of older days. Often they live alone and in many cases they do not possess full social and family status. They are confronted in their society with an anonymous, or at least a largely dehumanized, labor world on one hand, and on the other—as a sort of counterbalance—a world where the intimate life of marriage and family is valued more highly than ever.

Particularly difficult is the situation of men and women who have been left by their spouses or who are divorced. Those who never married have generally formed substantial lasting friendships within a social group, but these others are often totally alone and feel quite painfully the anomaly of their position. There is little doubt that the fate of the single person today, regardless of the cause of his single status, presents more psychological and sociological problems than in those days when an unmarried person was fully incorporated into a stable family in a relatively static community.

In this new situation, the testimony of celibacy, freely and joyfully chosen for the sake of the kingdom of heaven, is newly accented and of particular value, provided that it is not lived in an atmosphere of isolation from family and society. Many people who are deprived of marriage due to human factors can find support and orientation through the One who gave up marriage of His own free will. The testimony of those who follow Christ in celibacy can somehow discover for them, in a situation seemingly forced upon them, more possibilities for fulfillment in loving service than they could have thought possible. It can unfold for them their own personal *kairos*, and reveal how they can "use to the full this present time of salvation" (Eph. 5:8).

Celibacy for the sake of the kingdom contains within itself the power to build a community of salvation. The kingdom of heaven is the gathering call of divine love. When it will be fully revealed, there will be a perfect community of blessed love. The way to that perfection is through the expression of shared friendship with Christ in the community of His disciples.

Retreat into the desert, the life of a hermit,

may be a stage in the life of one who remains single for the sake of the kingdom of heaven, but it cannot be *the* final and classical realization of his vocation. Celibacy does, indeed, free from a constricting membership in a clan or family, insofar as the family is a purely worldly and social group. But one of the most precious fruits of religious celibacy is that cordial and strong fraternal love that establishes a new family: a family that, together with the Christian family but in its own way, reflects the blessed community of the saints and manifests the gathering power of the kingdom of God.

Today it must be understood more clearly than ever that free abstention from marriage does not mean the total renunciation of any family-type community. On the contrary, its task is to construct the most stable form of community and friendship, the community of disciples gathered around the Master. Those who remain single for the sake of the kingdom of heaven can thus offer to a world, whose depersonalized character demands the counterbalance of a truly personal community, the welcome message that one who is unmarried is not condemned to isolation. Due to his particular situation, he is called upon to work in a community entirely on faith and the love of Christ.

The celibate priest ought not to be only a friend, brother and father to all who need him. Even to achieve this goal he, too, needs the cordial friendship and community of his brothers. Less than ever before can monasteries be mere work communities with their own special rules, discipline and administration. They must not be perturbed by a pathological fear of false friendships or of close contact with their fellowmen. Rather, they should embody in those communities of disciples to which they belong, that cordial friendship for one another—and for all men—that testifies to the presence of the Divine Master.

On the basis of this very realization, we should be especially thoughtful of the involuntarily unmarried and the deserted spouses and widows. It is particularly those who stand in dire need of cordial friendship and social recognition. The founding of a congregation for widows and deserted women is one of the most daring attempts to contribute to the solution of this problem. Much more needs to be done. The attention of our parishes, of relatives and friends of these single people, of secular institutions and of religious people are all required to find answers to this problem. The testimony of happy and fruitful continence, which is in itself valuable, and the concrete realization of a community formed on this basis should, indeed, coincide with the concern and the many initiatives now developing in behalf of those leading a single life.

Celibacy in View of Today's Spirituality of Marriage

Religiously based celibacy has new aspects not only in view of the new structure of the family and the new, often painful, position of those leading a single life, but also in relation to today's new spirituality of marriage.

In the past, the family-group could develop into a power that impeded the joyful acceptance of the kingdom of heaven, or else, redeemed of its complacency, it could develop into an ideal embodiment of the community of salvation. It was part of the mission and testimony of those vowed to celibacy to prepare the way to this redeemed self-understanding.

Today, in an administrated and practically organized world, the intimate personal community between husband and wife and the immediate family has assumed a new significance. In this we sense the danger of concentrating all hopes on marriage as such, and of thus exposing more than ever to frustration, spiritual isolation and despondency, those who must do without marriage. Under these circumstances, celibacy for the sake of the kingdom of heaven also takes on a new significance in that—provided it is a convincing testimony of real freedom and true fulfillment— it liberates from unredeemed "flesh and blood" ties while it binds in loving communion through ties of the spirit.

If we find—as we do—that our present time is marked by an almost primitive worship of sexual fulfillment, as if it possessed redeeming power in itself, we also find that a deeper understanding of marriage as a vocation and as a way to sainthood has evolved. We may attribute this development in some degree to the testimony of celibacy understood in the truly Christian sense. But this new understanding of marriage is by no means a mere modification of monastic spirituality; it is a development in its own right, wherein Christian families strive for sainthood and testify to the presence of divine love.

The understanding of the unmarried state for the sake of the kingdom of God can profit from today's spirituality of marriage. The young people of today understand much more clearly than a few generations ago that the choice of a celibate life is religiously absurd if it is not accompanied, indeed preceded, by a high esteem for marriage and a proper understanding of the Christian vocation of marriage. Knowing how good marriage is, celibacy can never be misinterpreted as abstention from "sour grapes," but must be seen for what it really is: love-in-action, the wholehearted presentation to God of the firstfruits of the earth and all the energies of love.

Well-educated Christian spouses now know, from the unfolding teachings of the Church, that their fertility for the kingdom of heaven is in proportion to the genuine conjugal love that forms the root and the shape of their parental responsibility and love. Faced with this example, the unmarried will see more clearly than ever that the value of their testimony and the spiritual fruitfulness of their celibacy are decisively determined by the strength of their truly personal communion and by their cordial fraternal and paternal (or maternal) love for all the children of God.

Questions for Further Discussion

1. Discuss celibacy in terms of its essentials, that is, the call and gift of the Spirit accepted as a free personal choice, and distinguish that from conditions that result "from the necessities and circumstances of an era." Why is celibacy called "more blessed"?

2. What function has celibacy served in the history of the Church, particularly in time when the Church grew worldly?

3. What benefit does celibacy share with those who are single, especially for those who are not single by choice?

4. How can the difficult situation of the widowed or divorced or other unattached persons be helped?

5. What has today's spirituality of marriage added to the understanding of celibacy? What has the spirit of celibacy added to a true understanding of marriage?

XI
Conversion to Ecumenical Thinking and Acting

"The Lord of Ages wisely and patiently follows out the plan of His grace on behalf of us sinners. In recent times He has begun to bestow more generously upon divided Christians remorse over their divisions and a longing for unity. Everywhere, large numbers have felt the impulse of this grace. . . . " With these words, the *Decree on Ecumenism* (Art. 1) traces the ecumenical movement and its progress. It shows the Catholic Church sincerely repentant for past failures, as indicated by "a remarkable admission of guilt" and humble trust in God's mercy and grace. The decree describes "sincere remorse" as a special grace.

There is no doubt that the Church's active participation in the ecumenical movement must begin with the "Confiteor" in which we acknowledge our own fault instead of a self-righteous pointing to our separated brethren and their ecclesial communities. The more faithfully we respond to God's grace by a humble admission of our shortcomings and a courageous effort to rectify our errors, the more we can rely on the assistance of God's grace to enlighten other Christian communities to make their own admission of guilt.

Contrite Commitment to the Great Commandment

Love and unity are Our Lord's great commandment and final legacy. "The Church by her relationship with Christ is a kind of sacrament or sign of intimate union with God and of the unity of all mankind" (*Constitution on the Church*, Art. 1). In view of the mystery of Christ's Passion, death and Resurrection, Our Lord prays for His Apostles and all those who accepted the faith in consequence of their sermons and genuine testimony of unity: "I have given them the glory you gave to me, that they may be one as we are one. With me in them and you in me, may they be so completely one that the world will realize that it was you who sent me and that I have loved them as much as you loved me" (John 17:22-23).

In order to reconcile man with God and, at the same time, with his fellowmen, Jesus not only submitted Himself to the baptism of repentance at the banks of the Jordan, but likewise to the bloody baptism on the Cross. The act of atonement opens the way to unity. Christ carries on His shoulders the heavy burden of mankind's sinful past. In Christ's sacrifice of atonement we recognize the law of salvation: Guilt and sin must first be atoned before healing and a wholesome future may be expected. This truth finds special application to the ecumenical movement which is meant to lead Christians from strife and discord to full unity and an all-embracing charity.

The Council has made a remarkable admission of past errors and guilt on the part of the Catholic Church and its official representatives, not only in the *Decree on Ecumenism*, but also in the two conciliatory rites; namely, the interfaith prayer service of the pope with the observers to the Council in the Basilica of St. Paul, and in the contrite retraction of previous declarations of excommunication between Rome and Constantinople. However, the value of such expressions of contrition remains questionable if, due to the remoteness of past failures, they leave us completely untouched and unconcerned.

There is a hypocritical way of throwing stones at Innocent III, Boniface VIII, Leo X, and Alexander VI, while we feel comfortable in the ivory tower of our self-righteousness. Yet it makes excellent sense to ask forgiveness of our Christian brethren for all our faults and arrogance in defending these mistakes. Up until now we have not only rationalized these blunders but even continued to make them in one way or another. The Second Vatican Council does not permit an easy retreat into the past when the admission of guilt is concerned. It rather demands that, after a sincere examination of conscience, we contritely face our age, tainted with past and present burdens which have not been fully accepted and repaired. "Their primary duty is to make an honest and careful appraisal of whatever needs to be renewed and achieved in the Catholic household itself, in order that its life may bear witness more loyally and luminously to the teachings and ordinances which have been handed down from Christ through the Apostles" (*Decree on Ecumenism*, Art. 4). It is important to remember that popes, bishops and religious superiors are included in the body of the faithful. They are not standing aloft on a mighty baroque pulpit in order to castigate the faithful as the "others."

On the other hand, by "faithful" we understand all those who have faith. Consequently, when speaking of remorse, conversion and reform, we do not simply admit the faults of prelates. We all strike our own breasts as we humbly say: "My own fault." The appeal to repentance is addressed not only to the individuals, but also to the whole community of Christians. The Church, as a basic prerequisite to full conversion, must subject all its institutions, its liturgy, canon law, its administrative practices, its interpersonal relationships and its financial transactions, to a thorough and humble examination of conscience. In this respect, the *Decree on Ecumenism* is very clear and emphatic.

This new approach may shock those who hitherto have believed that their love and devotion to the Church obliged them to defend all actions of the Church and its institutions. "Every renewal of the Church essentially consists in an increase of fidelity to her own calling. Undoubtedly, this explains the dynamism of the movement toward unity. Christ summons the Church, as she goes her pilgrim way, to that continual reformation of which she always has need, insofar as she is an institution of men here on earth. Therefore, if the influence of events or of the times has led to deficiencies in conduct, in Church discipline, or even in the formulation of doctrine (which must be carefully distinguished from the deposit of faith itself), these should be appropriately rectified at the proper moment" (*Decree on Ecumenism,* Art. 6).

Consequently, in her acceptance of the ecumenical movement among Christianity, the Catholic Church commits herself to a soul-searching examination of conscience. The Church's institutions and practices must be measured against the criterion of the great commandment of love and the prayer of Our Lord "that they all may be one." This prayer for unity also embraces that part of Christianity which is still separated from the See of Peter. In this regard the Council states: "There can be no ecumenism worthy of the name without a change of heart" (*Decree on Ecumenism,* Art. 7).

Ecumenism as Expression
Of the Worship of God

A one-sided apologetic view which only recognizes light on one's own side of the fence, while it seeks indisputable night and darkness on the other side, is not merely an insurmountable obstacle to Christian unity. It is, above all, a sin against due worship of God. Self-righteousness tends to blind us to the wonderful works of God's grace in other Christian communities. Our failure to admit God's action in their behalf borders on blasphemy. The recognition and acknowledgment of all the good on the other side must lead us further than mere formal dialogue. Our ecumenical efforts become genuine, sincere, credible, and convincing only when we acknowledge their genuine witness to Christ.

The *Decree on Ecumenism* duly emphasizes this aspect: "Catholics must joyfully acknowledge and esteem the truly Christian endowments from our common heritage which are to be found among our separated brethren. It is right and salutary to recognize the riches of Christ and virtuous works in the lives of others who are bearing witness to Christ, sometimes even to the shedding of their blood. For God is always wonderful in His works and worthy of admiration. Nor should we forget that whatever is wrought by the grace of the Holy Spirit in the hearts of our separated brethren can contribute to our own edification" (*Decree on Ecumenism*, Art. 4). The reader will certainly not overlook the style and tone of the preface. This approach to the worship of God, and the acknowledgment of the workings of God in the separated or not yet fully returned Churches and ecclesial communities and their members, will make possible the much desired co-celebration of the Eucharist as a decisive sign of unity.

Basic Rules for the Ecumenical Dialogue

The ecumenical dialogue is based on the spirit of sincere contrition and genuine desire for true worship of God. Such an attitude will enable us to overcome our historical burden and undue feelings of guilt and self-righteousness. The way to unity will then lead us along the ecumenical dialogue — still to be learned — and along the path of united action in the service of the entire human family. The basic rules for the ecumenical dialogue may well be summarized as follows:

1. *Our foremost duty is concentration on the common heritage.*

The Council is setting an example. For the

greater part, the *Decree on Ecumenism* emphasizes the things which unite us before God. Our common heritage is indeed great. As to the Orthodox Churches, there is a common deposit of faith and worship of God. It is surprising that, in view of such a communion of faith, hope and worship, theologians and churchmen could focus their attention so one-sidedly, if not exclusively, on the few issues separating us. The age of controversial theology, which likewise exerted its unfavorable influence on the various theological schools within the Church, ended with the opening of the Second Vatican Council. The outcome and resulting changes are gratifying.

Young people of today look with suspicion on those few isolated theologians who insist on continuing the old controversial route. They, like lepers, shout with hollow voices from graves and burial vaults, while in their own opinion they are the "holy few." Their mere presence among us is sufficient reason for further penance to all Catholics. All ecumenically minded Catholics must clearly disavow all attitudes of controversy. They furthermore must cultivate the ecumenical style of dialogue when talking to these extreme conservatives. By our sincere efforts to gather the "red-hot coals" of our carefully collected energies of understanding love to spread on their heads (in their behalf), we shall be prepared for a more effective ecumenical dialogue not only with those friendly and open-minded, but also with those less receptive brothers and sisters among the various Christian communities still separated from us.

In my own experience I have found it most

distressing to listen to the petty complaints of some Monsignor who does not wish to accept the ecumenically minded and more humble Church of the Second Vatican Council as the Church of his choice. Similarly, I feel greater frustration when I am attacked by certain canonists who launch their attack from the well-protected battlements of their casuistry and hurl their accusations against various Protestant denominations and ecumenically minded theologians and bishops, than when I am subjected to unpleasant opposition from men and women of other Churches. One might ask the question whether there is greater openness among our Protestant and Orthodox brethren than among certain Catholic circles. We understand the deeply felt solidarity between the complaining Monsignor and the Catholic canonist, entrenched behind the letter of the law. Their common problem should remind us of our own shortcomings.

2. *Differences in perspectives and expressions are not separating walls but mutually enriching factors.*

Shortly before the beginning of the Second Vatican Council a famous ultraconservative archbishop of the Curia postulated that the foremost prerequisite for unity would be the acceptance of Thomistic philosophy as the sole philosophy of the Catholic Church. His syllogism was: If Thomism is true for the Dominicans, it must also be true for the Franciscans. If it is true for the West, it must also be true for the East. If it was true in the 13th century, then it must be equally true throughout all the

153

centuries to follow. The fault of his reasoning lies in the premise where "being true" is confused with "*the* truth"! Thomas Aquinas, together with his famous school, is not synonymous with *the* truth! He made a more or less successful attempt to answer in medieval language the philosophical questions of his own time. He is praiseworthy for his readiness to enter a dialogue with the religious currents of his age. He is classical because he was successful in drawing up formulations which even today vitally enrich our thinking.

The Council clearly dissociated itself from the idea that one theological or philosophical school should ever have a monopoly in the Church. Moreover, the Roman Catholic Church of the West, in her entire historical structure, steers away from such a monopoly in theological matters. Catholic unity means multiplicity. "Far from being an obstacle to the Church's unity, . . . diversity of customs and observances only adds to her comeliness. . . . To remove any shadow of doubt, then, this sacred Synod solemnly declares that the Churches of the East, while keeping in mind the necessary unity of the whole Church, have the power to govern themselves according to their own disciplines, since these are better suited to the temperament of their faithful. . . . Although it has not always been honored, the strict observance of this traditional principle is among the prerequisites for any restoration of unity. . . . What has already been said about legitimate variety we are pleased to apply to differences in theological expressions of doctrine" (*Decree on Ecumenism*, Art. 16, 17).

3. *Fruitful dialogue presupposes willingness to listen and to learn.*

The response from a leading voice in the conservative opposition at the Council to a brotherly invitation for dialogue in controversial issues was: "Do not expect me to enter into a dialogue in which I am expected to change something of what I am and what, in full allegiance to the will of God, I consider right."

It is understood that the Catholic Church in its ecumenical dialogue must neither deny its own identity, nor renounce its fidelity to God. Nevertheless, the Church must make a distinction between the things of God, that is, faithfulness to Divine Revelation and obedience to the divine will, on the one hand, and, on the other, the things which are prone to error as we search for God or are simply expressions of human weakness, limitation and sin. The Church would indeed deny its identity if she had no desire to rectify or to reform anything.

In a similar manner, as the theological schools within the Church are interdependent in their effort to safeguard Christian principles and prevent narrowness and one-sidedness, so also the partners in the ecumenical dialogue will mutually gain through their exchange of opinion. The Church will always hold to matters of revealed truth. Yet the ecumenical dialogue can help to express such truths in more intelligible ways and thereby aid the incorporation of these truths into the total view of faith and way of life. Humility, love of truth, and the willingness to learn should not only characterize the life of the individual theologian but also the entire Church as a community of salvation and faith.

The willingness and ability to listen and to learn is a decisive criterion of a truly "spiritual man." However, false conciliatory approaches, referred to as irenicism, must be avoided because they are harmful to the Catholic doctrine and obscure its genuine meaning (cf. *Decree on Ecumenism*, Art. 11).

Catholics, in their ecumenical dialogue, will particularly guard those truths of our common heritage which have not only been preserved faithfully but even developed with special care by our non-Catholic partners. Furthermore, when explaining certain typical aspects of Catholic doctrine, we should "remember that in Catholic teaching there exists an order or 'hierarchy' of truths, since they vary in their relationship to the foundation of the Christian faith" (*Decree on Ecumenism*, Art. 11). At the same time, "Catholic belief needs to be explained more profoundly and precisely, in ways and in terminology which our separated brethren can readily understand" (*Decree on Ecumenism*, Art. 11). Mutual patience and assistance among the Christian partners is a primary prerequisite for ecumenical dialogue. Our chief aim should be to make the Christian message more intelligible and understandable to modern man who is tempted by disbelief, or has fallen prey to atheism.

4. *The ecumenical dialogue must penetrate the entire Church.*

The "ecumenical movement" requires thoughtful preparation. In our efforts toward Christian unity, we must recognize our limitations. Even the most learned theologian will realize his limitations in competence because at times it is difficult to make clear distinctions and decisions. Knowledge, wisdom and humility usually go hand in hand.

Although the ecumenical dialogue between expert theologians of the different Churches and ecclesial communities is most important, every Christian has his share of responsibility in the ecumenical movement, that is, in fostering of unity among Christians. To accomplish this goal, the Council stipulates that the theological instructions for future shepherds and priests "must be presented from an ecumenical point of view" (*Decree on Ecumenism*, Art. 10). The decree then continues to give the reason for the above injunction by saying: "so that at every point they may more accurately correspond with the facts of the case." The *Decree on Priestly Formation* declares: "According to an opportune evaluation of the conditions of various regions, students should be led to a more adequate understanding of the Churches and ecclesial communities separated from the Roman, Apostolic See. Thus the students can contribute to the restoration of unity among all Christians according to the directives of this sacred Synod" (*Decree on Priestly Formation*, Art. 16). Recently, outstanding theology departments at Protestant-affiliated universities, in their desire for true ecumenical dialogue, have erected chairs for Catholic theologians. The author of these essays is fortunate to hold such chairs as visiting professor in three Protestant university departments.

Ecumenical Movement

As soon as ecumenical dialogue is established in which mutual respect and understanding predominates, Christians from different ecclesial communities will discover a considerable common heritage. In such dialogue they can jointly testify to a faith and to a hope that will not come to nought. Christian hope bears special witness in active love. "Since in our times cooperation in social matters is very widely practiced, all men without exception are summoned to united effort. Those who believe in God have stronger summons, but the strongest claims are laid on Christians, since they have been sealed with the name of Christ. Cooperation among all Christians vividly expresses that bond which already unites them, and it sets in clearer relief the features of Christ the Servant. . . . Through such cooperation, all believers in Christ are able to learn easily how they can understand each other better and esteem each other more, and how the road to the unity of Christians may be made smooth" (*Decree on Ecumenism*, Art. 12). The *Pastoral Constitution on the Church in the Modern World* similarly expresses this hope of cooperation for the benefit of all of mankind (cf. *Pastoral Constitution on the Church in the Modern World*, esp. Art. 89ff).

Common Prayer for Unity

The ecumenical movement is founded on the will of God as expressed in the farewell prayer of Jesus addressed to His disciples. The chief causes of separation are human weakness and sin. True contrition, which prepares the hearts for reunion, is a gift of God's grace. All the endeavors for unity should be penetrated by the conviction of man's weakness and the power of God's grace. This confident desire for ultimate unity finds fitting expression in prayer, as well as in an action, purified and strengthened by prayer. Hence it should be normal and logical that Christians from different communities try to gather for joint prayer services, especially those for unity. The Council expresses caution and a certain restraint because this is an entirely new territory for most Catholics. "In certain special circumstances, such as in prayer services 'for unity' and during ecumenical gatherings, it is allowable, indeed, desirable, that Catholics should join in prayer with their separated brethren. Such prayers in common are certainly a very effective means of petitioning for the grace of unity, and they are a genuine expression of the ties which even now bind Catholics to their separated brethren. 'For where two or three are gathered together for my sake, there am I in the midst of them' (Matt. 18:20)" (*Decree on Ecumenism*, Art. 8).

Our goal is worship in the fullness of community, namely, a common celebration of the Eucharist as the expression of unity in the one and only Church (cf. *Decree on Ecumenism*, Art. 4). One of the fundamental questions of ecumenism which arises today is: In what sense is the Eucharist a symbol of unity? Is it a static symbol of an already achieved unity or is it a dynamic sign of the powerful work of God to guide us in our decisive steps — a sign of our willingness, with God's grace, to contribute our share toward the achievement of this goal? The Council offers at least a practical hint for our guidance in the future: Although the ecclesial union with the Orthodox Churches has as yet not been fully achieved, the Council considers the possibility (even before mutual retraction of bulls of excommunication) of a certain worship in common, including the celebration of the Eucharist. This is not "merely possible, but is recommended" with the approval of the Church (cf. *Decree on Ecumenism*, Art. 15; cf. *Decree on Eastern Catholic Churches*, Art. 27).

The Eucharist is a symbol of unity. In order that its significance be more fully realized in a concelebrated liturgy, we need a certain degree of unity, although not unity at every point; for perfect unity as a reality can be realized only in heaven where all danger of discord has ceased. Careful theological work and prudent pastoral guidance by the hierarchy is required so that optimum requirements for common worship can be agreed upon. As the Christian communities draw closer in true ecumenical endeavors, this aspect needs constant reevaluation. It is self-evident that outdated rules, found in handbooks of morality and formulated in a time of unecumenical thinking and striving, must be replaced with new ecumenical thinking.

Questions for Further Discussion

1. Why does the idea of acknowledging our fault for past failures in the Church strike with such distaste in many hearts? What are some of these failures?

2. What would you say that you personally might have added to these failures? What can you do to remedy them?

3. Discuss the basic rules the author gives for ecumenical dialogue. Do these appear "new" or startling to you? Why or why not?

4. Why are differences in insights and expression to be valued rather than scorned? Can you give some important but allowable differences between the major religions? Between Catholic and Orthodox? Between different theological and philosophical schools of thought?

5. Discuss some specific ways of promoting common prayer for unity in your diocese.

XII

Blessed Are the Peacemakers

The messianic hope of God's people in the Old Testament can be summarized in one word: peace. The resurrected Christ offers His Apostles peace as His greeting and gift. He sends them out as messengers of the messianic peace. The Law of the New Covenant praises the children of peace, those who receive peace from the Lord and who make peace, those who carry peace in their hearts and negotiate peace (cf. Matt. 5:9). They are the true sons and daughters of God.

With this in mind, some clear distinctions must be made. The messianic expectation, as expressed in many utterances of the Apostles before Pentecost, was too much an expectation of a purely earthly kingdom of power and peace. At the other extreme were those pietists who could be found in almost any community, pietists concerned only with their own peace of mind and who felt no challenge, on the basis of this, to spread peace among men. The "peace of the Lord" is neither of these.

The messianic peace is a gift that comes to life in the heart of the disciple of Christ in the midst of what may be a rather stormy life. It is a reality that extends far beyond the vicissitudes of this life. The true disciple of Christ is rooted firmly in his faith and in his hope for the messianic peace even when the world is torn with dissension and war. The messianic peace is a fruit of the Holy Spirit, a gift from above which can be asked and received only in humility. But where this fruit of the Spirit is truly received, there it will bear fruit; it will radiate peace. One cannot be a son or daughter of God without promoting peace in one's own world, one's environment, and to the extent of one's own abilities. A Christian's acceptance of the message of peace is indivisible.

Christ, the Prince of Peace

"That earthly peace which arises from the love of neighbor symbolizes and results from the peace of Christ who comes forth from God the Father. For by His cross the Incarnate Son, the Prince of Peace, reconciled all men with God. By thus restoring the unity of all men in one people and one body, He slew hatred in His own flesh. After being lifted on high by His Resurrection, He poured the Spirit of love into the hearts of men" (*Pastoral Constitution on the Church in the Modern World,* Art. 78).

The great peace program with which the last document of the Second Vatican Council concludes is built around the commitment to Christ as the Prince of Peace. Unless my eyes deceive me, the future of the world and largely of Christianity also, will be decided by whether all men of good will are going to cooperate energetically in making this program work. An examination of conscience about the contribution to peace on all levels cannot be absent from any Christian catechism of the future.

Our Christian mission in regard to peace on earth must begin with the endeavor to know Christ, the Prince of Peace, better. His coming to earth is a message of peace to all men of good will, to all men through whom the gracious kindness of God is revealed. It is a message which first reaches the poor (cf. Luke 2:8-20). Christ's messianic office means a particular proximity to the poor and oppressed. He has come to "set the downtrodden free, to proclaim the Lord's year of favor" (Luke 4:18-19). Christ did not come to be judge over matter of law. But He brings peace on every level wherever His message finds acceptance. "He will . . . turn the hearts of fathers toward their children and the disobedient back to the wisdom that the virtuous have, preparing for the Lord a people fit for him" (Luke 1-17).

Concord and union among His disciples are a sign of Christ's presence among them. He sends forth His disciples to announce and to bring peace to every house; so much so that the Apostle of the Peoples can say, "He is the peace between us" (Eph. 2:14). This he says with reference to the calling of all people and all men to the kingdom of peace. The new people of God must recognize no wall between Jews and pagans. He made peace "through the cross to unite them both in a single body and reconcile them with God. In his own person he killed hostility" (Eph. 2:15). When the disciples accept the gift and the calling of all-embracing love from the Lord, then the blessing of Col. 3:15 is directed to them: "May the peace of Christ reign in your hearts, because it is for this that you were called together as parts of *one* body."

The Message of Peace and the Courage of Division

The peace message of Christ must not be belittled. It must be envisioned with all its heights, depths and tensions. Jesus tells His disciples, "Peace I bequeath you, my own peace I give you, a peace the world cannot give, this is my gift to you" (John 14:27). However, he who desires the peace of Christ must follow Him in the decisive "no" to any form of unsound peace. This is expressed with utmost urgency in the word: "Do you suppose that I am here to bring peace on earth? No, I tell you, but rather division" (Luke 12:51).

Just as Jesus Himself became a nuisance to the Pharisees and scribes and just as He took the consequences upon Himself, the disciple, too, must persevere in his mission to bring peace, even though it might bring him disgrace and suffering. The best test of the messianic peacemaker lies in the love for his enemies. "Alas for you when the world speaks well of you! This was the way their ancestors treated the false prophets. But I say this to you who are listening: Love your enemies, do good to those who hate you, bless those who curse you, pray for those who treat you badly" (Luke 6:26-28). These central words of the Sermon on the Mount show the strength and the power of the messianic peace. The disciple of Christ whose heart is filled with the peace of Christ cannot be embittered by anything. The concentrated power of love that embodies and announces the messianic peace proves its worth in the attitude of genuine nonviolence. Yet this must not be interpreted as mere abstention from violent measures. Only that inner strength is decisive that overcomes evil by doing good.

Temptation will forever exist in the desire to

dissolve the polarity—one might almost say the contrastive harmony—in favor of the one pole. A wrong irenicism will deny the testimony to the truth—be it "peace" with those in power in one's own Church or peace with the currents of the day —while infuriated fanatics would force a victory for truth with the help of the stake. The one pays for his peace with indifferentism to the search for truth, the other with indifferentism to truth and love. The one becomes a pacifist because of apathy and timidity in the cause of justice, the other is willing to defend the just cause, as he sees it, with every possible means, even to the point where none of those who were in need of justice will survive in the end.

The disciple of Christ can fight the battle for His true peace only with the weapon of love. He who wants to fight at the forefront of peace must be well equipped with love and the strength of the peace of Christ. He who wants to spread and establish peace among men must be ready to pay its price. An easy pacifism has nothing in common with the Gospel. To those, however, who are quick with their sword, it is said: "Put your sword back, for all who draw the sword will die by the sword" (Matt. 26:52). Neither the spiritual nor the worldly sword furthers the cause of Christ and of peace among men when enthusiasm for justice is not matched with the persevering strength of a love that endures and hopes everything.

Dialectical materialism breaks up the synthesis of the desired peace into a thesis and antithesis of hatred and struggle. A redemption of Marxism will be possible only if Christians succeed in making credible, with great love and with the willingness to make sacrifices, the synthesis of courageous sacrifice for truth and justice and a love that overcomes every obstacle.

Indivisibility of Peace

Christ is not only the redeemer of souls; He is also the Redeemer and the Lord of the world. The truly redeemed, those who accept the gift of redemption with an undivided heart and with all their faith, become messengers of and witnesses to peace on all levels and in all the different areas of life.

Ecumenism is an acceptance of Christ's commandment to make peace. Christians must bury their swords in their search for the full truth of Christ, if they want to draw nearer to the truth of God and if they want to become credible heralds of the peace of Christ among all nations. The feud between different schools of theologians which has done much damage to truth and salvation must not be supplanted by even fiercer feuds between the progressives and conservatives. The existence of different schools is justified only if it is an expression of a common search, a dialogue in love, and unity in diversity. Very different degrees of progressivism and concern for the preservation of a precious heritage do no harm to the Church if everyone concerned endures in his testimony to the messianic peace, not only in spite of but actually because of the presence of diversity.

Concern for the peace of Christ must particularly characterize marriage and family life. Relatives and neighbors, one's job, the relationship between employer and employee, union and entrepreneur, parties and nations are all realms where the messianic peace should be reflected through the efforts and the testimony of Christian men and women. No area must be left out, for everything is created, redeemed and directed toward Him who is called the Prince of Peace. The messianic peace does not shelter us in a glass house; rather it sends us forth into the world, frequently to the most stormy places in the world. A Christian must never be entangled in the hatred of the world. Yet he must be "entangled," that is, committed to the struggle of mankind for peace and justice.

Not all men can do everything. Each one of us is called upon to serve the undivided peace with his talents and in his place. One person has the charism to further peace in the ecclesial realm, in his parish, in his order, or in his diocese, between liberals and conservatives, between clergy and laymen. However, he will never seek a peace that would shut the doors, for instance, to ecumenism, the peace of all Christianity. He will not be able to achieve peace for the price of an officially ordered disinterest for social justice or of a betrayal of the integration of the discriminated. Another person will have the charism to stand up against narrow-mindedness and fanatical intolerance among the ranks of his own Church or his own party. Yet he cannot be sure of his charism unless he possesses a goodly amount of humor and unless he knows how to combine a word of reconciliation with a gentle "nudge in the ribs." Whoever lacks humor might better look for another field and another object for his pacification efforts.

Everyone who has something to do with the business world must contribute somehow to social peace. Everyone who is eligible to vote can somehow serve the cause of justice and of peace with his ballot. Those who have a charism for making peace, because of the gifts of God and of their position, must become heralds of mutual understanding, of justice in mutual respect. The professional politician has a special calling to serve the peace between parties, interest groups and nations. A Christian who has all the necessary qualifications for a political career will not say, "I might soil my hands." Rather, he will gratefully welcome such an extraordinary opportunity to serve the cause of peace in his world and in his time. The journalist, the editor, the commentator also have special responsibilities in the matter of social and international peace, for whether nations will come closer and whether politicians will be forced to think thoughts of peace depends greatly upon public opinion, the formation of which these people can effectively influence. There is no one who cannot make his modest yet indispensable contribution to peace, if only through his respectful attitude toward other nations and members of other races and religions.

The Theory of the Just War

The history of Christianity shows, besides great prophets of the messianic peace, also men of the sword. The Christians range from those enthusiastic crusaders who took the sack of Constantinople upon their consciences, to a Francis of Assisi who called on the Sultan with the gospel of love as his sole weapon. Among the theologians there were great heralds of peace as well as patient defenders of the just war. But the conditions and the theory of the "just war" cannot be lumped together indiscriminately, as was frequently the case in the past. The conditions for a just war were worked out so penetratingly by some theologians that a conscientious Christian who trusted those theologians lost all desire to volunteer for military service. Those conditions for a just war were meant to curb the military ambitions of the princes. Frequently it was the most feasible method of checking war in the historical situation. Yet it cannot be denied that other moralists did not weigh the conditions for a "just war" too carefully. There were almost always princes of the Church on both sides who were all too eager to bless weapons and armies and to curse those of the other side.

Pope John XXIII, in his encyclical *Pacem in Terris* (Peace on Earth), and the Second Vatican Council, in its chapter on the "Fostering of Peace and the Promotion of a Community of Nations," continue in the tradition of those theologians and heralds of peace who drew up so many conditions to the possibility of a just war that a justification of war became close to impossible. The following sentence ought to be understood with this in mind: "Certainly, war has not been rooted out of human affairs. As long as the danger of war remains and there is no competent and sufficiently powerful authority at the international level, governments cannot be denied the right to legitimate defense, once every means of peaceful settlement has been exhausted" (*Pastoral Constitution on the Church in the Modern World,* Art. 79). One must not, by any means, take this sentence apart from the rather sharp condemnation of any form of total war, any war of aggression, or any meaningless defensive war.

However, the Second Vatican Council does not limit itself at all to stipulating more up-to-date conditions for a just war. It praises those who "renounce the use of violence in the vindication of their rights" (*Pastoral Constitution on the Church in the Modern World,* Art. 78). The Council unmasks the threat of war as a consequence of man's sinfulness and it announces the hope for peace as the fruit of conversion: "But to the extent that men vanquish sin by a union of love, they will vanquish violence as well, and make these words come true: 'They shall beat their swords into plowshares and their spears into pruning hooks; one nation shall not raise the sword against another, nor shall they train for war again' (Isa. 2:14)" (*Pastoral Constitution on the Church in the Modern World,* Art. 78).

The Council is definitely aware of the intricacy of the situation, yet it makes clear to everyone that the situation is infinitely serious. It is possible that mankind is already close to ridding itself of this maniac belief that wars are necessary. "Divine Providence urgently demands of us that we free ourselves from the age-old slavery of war. But if we refuse to make this effort, we do not know where the evil road we have ventured upon will lead us" (*Pastoral Constitution on the Church in the Modern World,* Art. 81).

Some pacifists were disappointed by the texts of the Council. They expected a clear, unequivocal condemnation of any form of war. They clamored for the loudest trumpets of justice and judgment. However, the critics overlook the fact that the Council did not limit itself to speaking against war. Its decisive message is that it points out the way to peace. Yet this demands much more of every individual and of all nations than a comfortable pacifism that is satisfied with a mere condemnation of war. He who wants peace must pool his energies with the common efforts for peace.

The untiring sermons for peace and the peace efforts of Pope Paul are completely in line with the peace program of the Council. The establishment of a special secretariat for the fostering of justice and peace is a promising beginning that lets us hope that more and more Christians will realize how the messianic peace, the salvation promised us by Christ, demands a new attitude and steady efforts for peace on all levels.

The upbringing of our youth and the education of adults must focus on all the implications of the Christian peace mission. It must be universally realized how absurd it is to speak either of a "just war" or of absolute pacifism when the furthering of social peace, of justice, and friendship among nations is not given due attention, and when the necessary sacrifices for peaceful settlement, order and reconciliation of all nations are not made.

Questions for Further Discussion

1. Distinguish the "peace of the Lord" from its many counterfeits.

2. What are the implications in the author's statement that "the future of the world and largely of Christianity also will be decided by whether all men of good will are going to cooperate energetically" in making the peace program built upon Christ as the Prince of Peace work?

3. What does the statement that Luke put on the lips of Christ mean: "Do you suppose that I am here to bring peace on earth? No, I tell you, but rather division" (Luke 12:51)?

4. Discuss the "peacemaker" in various walks of life. In your own.

5. What is the theory of the "just war"? Is it relevant today? What did the Council propose as a counterforce to war?

CARMELITE MONASTERY
Beckley Hill
Barre, Vt., 05641

DATE BORROWED